Introduction
to Ox

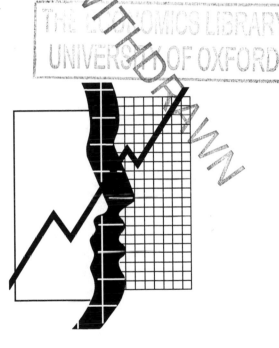

Introduction
to Ox

Jurgen A. Doornik,

Gerrit Draisma,

Marius Ooms

Timberlake Consultants Ltd
A Leading Distributor of Statistical and Econometric Software

Introduction To Ox

Copyright © 1998 Jurgen A. Doornik, Gerrit Draisma, Marius Ooms

British Library Cataloguing-in-Publication Data
A catalogue record for this book is available from the British Library

First edition 1998, published by Timberlake Consultants Press a Division of Timberlake Consultants Ltd.

Printed in the UK by Allstar Services, Harrow

Cover designed in the UK by CCA Design and Communications Ltd., London

ISBN 0-9533394-1-6

Timberlake Consultants Ltd
47 Hartfield Crescent
West Wickham
Kent
BR4 9DW
U.K.
http://www.timberlake.co.uk

Contents

Preface

This is a hands-on introduction to the Ox programming language. It may be used for self study, or in a classroom setting with an instructor. Exercises are spread throughout the text, both to check and extend the understanding of the language. Some more extensive exercises are given, which may be set as take home tests for students (for example, the questions at the end of Chapter 10). Not all details of the language are discussed here; for more information we refer to Doornik (1998), which contains a full reference of the Ox language.

We hope that a working knowledge of the material in this booklet will allow you to use Ox more productively, whether in your studies or research. Please let us know if you have any comments on this introduction.

It is assumed that you have a copy of Ox installed on your machine and working. If not, you can download a copy from *http://www.nuff.ox.ac.uk/Users/Doornik*.

Some conventions are used in this book. Source code, variables in source code and file names are written in `typewriter` font. Exercises are indicated with a ▶ in the margin, and referred to as [3.1] (for example), where 3 is the chapter number, and 1 the exercise number in that chapter. Sections are referred to as e.g. §3.1. Source code is listed between dotted lines. For many of these the code is provided to save typing. In that case, the right-hand side of the top dotted line gives the filename in *italics*. All the files will have the .ox extension, although some of those will not be valid Ox code as such (the file is always an exact copy of the code in the text, and occasionally this is only part of a program).

We wish to thank Francisco Cribari-Neto for helpful comments.

Jurgen Doornik
Gerrit Draisma
Marius Ooms

Chapter 1

Ox Environment

1.1 Installing Ox

We assume that you have access to a properly installed version of Ox. If you do not have Ox yet, you can download a copy from *http://www.nuff.ox.ac.uk/Users/Doornik*. Or contact Timberlake Consultants. Timberlake can be found on the internet at `www.timberlake.co.uk` and `www.timberlake-consultancy.com`, or contacted via telephone in the UK on: +44 (0)181 462 0495/0093, and in the US on: +1 415 924 3085.

1.2 Ox version

You can follow these tutorials using Ox version 2.00 or newer, on any available computer platform.

1.3 Running an Ox program

All versions of Ox which are free for educational purposes are *console versions*. This means that the program is launched from the command line in a console window (e.g. from the MS-DOS command prompt in a Dos window). Output will appear on the console as well.

To run an Ox source code file called `myfirst.ox`, issue the command (the `.ox` extension need not be typed):

command	platform
`oxl myfirst.ox`	Windows NT/95 console
`oxdos myfirst.ox`	MS-DOS/Windows 3.1 console
`oxl myfirst.ox`	most Unix consoles

▶[1.1] We suggest that you now try to run an Ox program:
    (1) Open an MS-DOS command prompt window.

1

(2) Go to the Ox folder (this *could* be `C:\Program files\Ox` under Windows 95/NT, and `C:\ProgramF\Ox` under Windows 3.1 or MS-DOS).

(3) Go to the `samples` folder (directory).

(4) Run the command (under old MS-DOS and windows 3.1 use the `oxdos` command):

```
oxl myfirst
```

The output should be (the version of Ox could be newer):

```
Ox version 2.00 (Windows) (C) J.A.Doornik, 1994-98
two matrices
        2.0000        0.00000        0.00000
        0.00000       1.0000         0.00000
        0.00000       0.00000        1.0000

        0.00000       0.00000        0.00000
        1.0000        1.0000         1.0000
```

If the output is:

```
myfirst.ox (1): 'oxstd.h' include file not found
myfirst.ox (7): 'unit' undeclared identifier
myfirst.ox (11): 'print' undeclared identifier
```

then your include variable is not yet set (see §A1.1).

If the output is something like 'bad command or filename', your path is not set (again see §A1.1).

If `oxl` works, that is the preferred program (instead of `oxdos`), together with OxRun, as discussed below.

1.4 Redirecting output

Output from the console version appears on the console. To capture it in a file, *redirect* the output, e.g. to `myprog.out` as in:

```
oxl myfirst.ox > myprog.out
```

The `more` command may be used to page through large amounts of output (but you may prefer to use an editor):

```
oxl myfirst.ox | more
```

1.5 Help and documentation

The reference book for the Ox language is Doornik (1998). Much of that is also available in the online help. This help system is in the form of HTML documents, which can be read with an internet browser such as Netscape or the Internet Explorer. The help files can be found in the `ox\doc` directory; the master file is `index.htm`. To read the file in the Internet Explorer, choose File/Open, then browse to find `index.htm`, and then open it. The entries at the top give access to the *table of contents*, and to the *index*. The capture below shows the help on `rank`.

►[1.2] Open the help system in your browser. Use the index to find help on the `rows()` function. Explore other functions and other parts of the help system. You may also use the browser's find command to search in the open document.

1.6 Using the OxEdit editor

A powerful editor for use with Ox, called *OxEdit*, is available for use with Ox. OxEdit supports syntax colouring of Ox programs, making them more readable, and reducing the incidence of typing errors. You can also install Ox within OxEdit, so that programs can be run from within the editor, and output captured in a text window. Some additional information and a screen capture is given in §A1.2. OxEdit works under Windows 95 (or newer) and NT, but *not* under Windows 3.1.

1.7 Using GiveWin via OxRun

Ox can also interact with GiveWin. If you use OxRun to run the program, the output (both text and graphics) will appear in GiveWin. The following capture shows how to use OxRun to run `myfirst.ox`, with some graphics and text output from ox\samples\simula\simnor.ox in the background. If the include variable is set as for the console version, then the Include edit field can be left empty. OxRun can also run programs from the command line. In addition, it can run interactively, and run as a debugger of Ox programs.

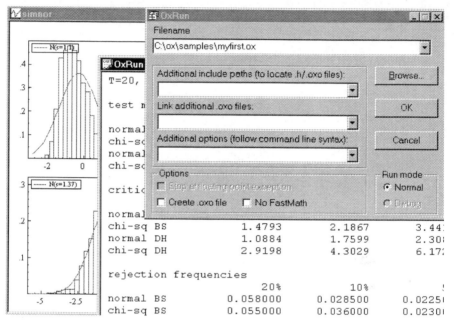

1.8 Graphics

Graphics is discussed in Chapter 6.

1.9 Compilation and run-time errors

Program statements are processed in two steps, resulting in two potential types of errors:

(1) Compilation errors

The statements are scanned in and compiled into some kind of internal code. Errors which occur at this stage are compilation errors. No statements are executed when there is a compilation error. Compilation errors could be caused by undeclared variables, wrong number of function arguments, forgetting a semicolon at the end of a statement (among many other reasons). For example, these two messages are caused by one undeclared variable at line 10 of the program:

```
D:\Waste\myfirst.ox (10): 'y' undeclared identifier
D:\Waste\myfirst.ox (10): lvalue expected
```

Occasionally, a syntax errors leads to a large list of error messages. Then, correcting the first mistake could well solve most of the problem.

(1) Run-time errors

When the code which does not have syntax errors is executed, things can still go wrong, resulting in a run-time error. An example is trying to multiply two matrices which have non matching dimension. Here, this happened at line 10 in the main function:

```
Runtime error: 'matrix[3][3] * matrix[2][3]' bad operand
Runtime error occurred in main(10), call trace:
D:\Waste\myfirst.ox (10): main
```

1.10 A debug session

Ox has debug facilities, which can be useful to locate bugs in your programs. A debug session is started with the -d switch (use oxli.exe under Windows). When debugging you can:

- inspect the contents of variables;
- change the value of variables;
- set or clear a break point at a source code line;
- trace through the code step by step;
- trace by stepping over a function call;
- trace into a function call (the function must be written in Ox code, not a library function).

When in debug mode, the prompt is given as (debug). The commands are:

```
#break file line   - set breakpoint at line of file
#clear file line   - clear breakpoint at line of file
#clear all         - clear all breakpoints
#go                - run to next breakpoint
#go file line      - run to line of file
#go line           - run to line of current file
?                  - debug command summary (also: #help)
??                 - show all symbols and current break
?symbol            - show a symbols
#quit              - stop debugging
#step in           - step (in to function) (also: press return)
#step over         - step (over function)
#step out          - step out of current function
#show              - shows current break
#show calls        - show call stack
#show variable     - same as ?variable
#show breaks       - show all breakpoints
#show all          - show all variables
#show full         - show all variables with full value
#trace             - lists all lines executed
```

```
#trace off            - switches trace off
!command              - operating system command
expression            - enter an Ox expression,
                        e.g. x[0][0]=1; or print(x);
```

Here is a session with `myfirst.ox`. The bold text is entered at the prompt. First we list the program being debugged (`samples/myfirst.ox`), with line numbers in bold in the margin.

1   `#include <oxstd.h>// include the Ox standard library header`

3   `main()                  // function main is the starting point`
4   `{`
5   `decl m1, m2;         // declare two variables, m1 and m2`

7   `m1 = unit(3);    // assign to m1 a 3 x 3 identity matrix`
8   `m1[0][0] = 2;                   // set top-left element to 2`
9   `m2 = <0,0,0;1,1,1>;// m2 is a 2x3 matrix, the first row`
                                  `// consists of zeros, the second of ones`

12   `print("two matrices", m1, m2);     // print the matrices`
13   `}`

```
C:\ox\samples> oxli -d myfirst
Entering debug mode, use #quit to quit, ? for help.
myfirst.ox (5): break!

(debug) #break 9
(debug) #go
myfirst.ox (9): break!
(debug) ??
=== local symbols ===
    0  m1[3][3]                 matrix    2 ...
    1  m2                       (null)

myfirst.ox (9): break!
(debug) ?m1
m1[3][3]                     matrix
        2.0000         0.00000        0.00000
        0.00000        1.0000         0.00000
        0.00000        0.00000        1.0000
(debug) m1[1][1] = -20;
(debug) ?m1
m1[3][3]                     matrix
        2.0000         0.00000        0.00000
        0.00000       -20.000         0.00000
        0.00000        0.00000        1.0000
(debug)
myfirst.ox (12): break!
(debug)
two matrices
        2.0000         0.00000        0.00000
        0.00000       -20.000         0.00000
```

```
    0.00000        0.00000        1.0000

    0.00000        0.00000        0.00000
    1.0000         1.0000         1.0000
myfirst.ox (13): break!
(debug) #quit
C:\ox\samples>
```

- **#break 9** sets a breakpoint at line 9 of the current source file.
- **#go** runs the program until a break is encountered.
- **??** lists all the variables which are visible within the current scope. We can see that m1 is a 3 × 3 matrix (element 0, 0 is also given); m2 has not been assigned a value yet, and is listed as (null).
- **?m1** prints the m1 variable. Only variable names are allowed after the question mark. To print part of a matrix use print, e.g. print(m1[0][1:]);.
- **m1[1][1] = -20;** changes the second diagonal element. The code must be valid Ox code, so do not forget the terminating semicolon!
- Just pressing enter does one step in the code, leading to line 12. The next enter runs to line 13, executing the print statement in the code.
- **#quit** aborts the debug session.

1.11 Have you programmed before?

If not, there is a lot to learn initially: not just a new language but also basic programming concepts which take some time to master. Some persistence is required too: a compiler (that is the program which runs your computer program) is unforgiving. Forget a comma here, or a semicolon there, and your program will not work at all.

Before continuing it is useful to ask the following question: do I need to solve problems which require Ox? If the main objective is regression analysis, then there will be several menu-driven programs (such as, e.g., PcGive) which are easier to use. But, if you need to do something slightly different, or do very extensive computations, Ox can be a powerful tool to solve the problem.

If you decide to use Ox and work through this tutorial, you will learn about programming and about Ox. Because of its simplicity and similarity to C, C++and Java, this is not a bad place to start. Moreover, you can immediately apply it to more relevant subject matter (econometrics, statistics, etc.).

As you will see in the upcoming chapters, the basic building blocks of an Ox computer program are *variables* and *functions* (sometimes called procedures or subroutines). A variable is like a box in which you can store a number. A function is like a recipe: it takes some variables as inputs (the ingredients), and gives output back. The purpose of a function is to isolate tasks which have to be used several times. Functions also help to break a program down in more manageable blocks. Finally, the complete program is all the variables and functions put together.

Chapter 2

Syntax

2.1 Introduction

This chapter gives a brief overview of the main syntax elements of the Ox language. Ox resembles C and C++ (and also Java), so if you're familiar with these languages, you'll recognize the format for loops, functions, etc. The most important differences are:

- The *matrix* is a standard type in Ox. You can work directly with matrices, for example adding or multiplying two matrices together. Ox also has the standard scalar types for integers (type int), and real numbers (type double).
  A vector is a matrix with one column or one row, whereas a 1×1 matrix is often treated as a scalar. Ox will keep track of matrix dimensions for you.
- Variables are *implicitly typed*. So a variable can start as an integer, then become a 10×1 matrix, then a 2×2 matrix. and so on. As in most languages, variables must be *explicitly declared*.
- Ox has strings and arrays as built-in types, to allow for higher dimensional matrices, or arrays of strings.

2.2 Comment

Ox has two types of comment: / * ... * / for blocks of comment, and / / for comment up to the end of a line:

```
. . . . . . . . . . . . . . . . . . . . . . . . . . . . . . . . . . . . . . . . . . . . . . . . . . . . . . . . . . . . . . . . .
/*
    This is standard comment, which /* may be nested */.
*/
decl x;  // declare the variable x
. . . . . . . . . . . . . . . . . . . . . . . . . . . . . . . . . . . . . . . . . . . . . . . . . . . . . . . . . . . . . . . . .
```

When writing functions, it is useful to add comment to document the function, especially the role of the arguments, and the return value. A useful template could be (here used for the library function olsc):

8

```
...................................................... oxtut2a
/*
** olsc(const mY, const mX, const amB);
**      mY        in:  T x n matrix Y
**      mX        in:  T x k matrix X
**      amB       in:  address of variable
**                out: k x n matrix with OLS coefficients
**
** Return value
**      integer: 1: success, 2: rescaling advised,
**          -1: X'X is singular, -2: combines 2 and -1.
**
** Description
**      Performs OLS, expecting the data in columns.
**
** Example
**      error = ols(my, mx, &mb);
**
** Last changed
**      21-04-96 (Marius Ooms): made documentation
*/
........................................................
```

If you use this template, you can do a find in files (called grep in Unix systems) to create a listing of all documentations. It may be useful to create a copy of this template for later use. Good documentation is important: often, it is better to have documentation and no code, than the other way round.

2.3 Program layout

The smallest complete program is:

```
...................................................... oxtut2b
#include <oxstd.h>

main()
{
}
........................................................
```

This program does nothing, but is worth discussing anyway:

- The first line includes a *header file*.   The contents of the file oxstd.h are literally inserted at the point of the #include statement. The name is between < and > to indicate that it is a *standard* header file: it actually came with the Ox system. The purpose of that file is to declare all standard library functions, so that they can be used from then onwards.
- This short program has one *function*, called main. It has no arguments, hence the empty parentheses (these are compulsary). An Ox program starts execution

at the `main` function; without `main`, there might be a lot of code, but nothing will happen.
- A block of code (here the empty *function body*), is enclosed in curly braces.

2.4 Statements

Statements are commands to do something, some computation for example. Important ingredients of statements are variables, to store or access a result, and operators (discussed in the next chapter) to combine existing results into new ones. A statement is terminated with a semicolon (`;`). Please note when you're copying code from paper: Ox makes a distinction between lower case and upper case letters.

```
....................................................... oxtut2c
#include <oxstd.h>

main()
{
    decl n, sigma, x, beta, eps;

    n = 4;   sigma = 0.25;
    x = 1 ~ ranu(n, 2);
    beta = <1; 2; 3>;

    eps = sigma * rann(n, 1);

    print("x", x, "beta", beta, "epsilon", eps);
}
.................................................................
```

Some remarks on this program:
- `decl` is used to declare the variables of this program.
- `n = 4` simply assigns the value 4 to the variable `n`.
- `print` is a standard library function used for printing.
- `*` multiplies two variables.
- `~` concatenates two variables. Here we concatenate an integer with a 4×2 matrix. The process can be pictured as:

$$
1 \sim \begin{pmatrix} x & x \\ x & x \\ x & x \\ x & x \end{pmatrix} \Rightarrow \begin{pmatrix} 1 & x & x \\ 1 & x & x \\ 1 & x & x \\ 1 & x & x \end{pmatrix}.
$$

▶[2.1] Run this Ox program. All the program listings which have a name on the right in the dotted line are made available. If you do not already have them, you can download then from `www.nuff.ox.ac.uk/users/doornik`. In this case the file is called `oxtut2c.ox`. By default, all these files live in `ox/tutorial`.

►[2.2] Use the help system to discover the meaning of `ranu` and `print`.

►[2.3] Add a line for computing $y = X\beta + \epsilon$. Also print the value of y. This requires:
  (1) `declaring` the variable `y`
  (2) inserting a statement computing $X\beta + \epsilon$ and storing it in `y`
  (3) adding a statement to `print` the `y` variable.

►[2.4] The `rows()` and `sizer()` functions returns the number of rows of a matrix, the `columns()` and `sizec()` functions the number of columns. Add a print statement to report the dimensions of `x` in the above program.

Here are some of the things which can go wrong in the previous exercises:

(1) Forget a comma. For example `decl a, b c;` needs a comma after the b.
(2) Forget a semicolon. For example `n = 4 sigma = 0.25;` has a semicolon missing.
(3) Adding a semicolon after the function header, as in:
```
main();
{
    // code
}
```
(4) Omitting the curly braces, as in:
```
main()
        print("some text");
```
(5) Forget to declare a variable. The new `y` variable must be declared before it can be used.
(6) Using the wrong case: `print(X);` would not work, because the variable is called `x`, not `X`.
(7) Any typo, such as writing `priny` instead of `print`.
(8) Matrix dimensions do not match in multiplication:

$$\begin{pmatrix} x & x & x \\ x & x & x \\ x & x & x \\ x & x & x \end{pmatrix} * \begin{pmatrix} x \\ x \end{pmatrix} \text{ fails, but } \begin{pmatrix} x & x & x \\ x & x & x \\ x & x & x \\ x & x & x \end{pmatrix} * \begin{pmatrix} x \\ x \\ x \end{pmatrix} \text{ works.}$$

2.5 Identifiers

Identifiers (names of variables and functions) may be up to 60 characters long. They may consist of the characters [A-Z], [a-z], [_], and [0-9], but may not start with a digit.

2.6 Style

It is useful to raise the issue of programming style at this early stage. A consistent style makes a program more readable, and easier to extend. Even in the very small programs of these tutorials it helps to be consistent. Often, a program of a few lines grows over time as functionality is added. With experience, a good balance between conciseness and clarity will be found.

Here is one solution to the previous exercise:

```
#include <oxstd.h>

main()
{
    decl n, sigma, x, y, beta, eps;

    n = 4;   sigma = 0.25;
    x = 1 ~ ranu(n, 2);
    beta = <1; 2; 3>;

    eps = sigma * rann(n, 1);
    y = x * beta + eps;

    print("x", x, "beta", beta, "epsilon", eps);
    print("y", y);
    print("x has ", rows(x), " rows and ",
        columns(x), " columns\n");
}
```

But this solution will work too:

```
#include <oxstd.h>
main()
{decl n,x1,x,y,x2,x3;
n=4;x1=0.25;x=1~ranu(n,2);
x2=<1;2;3>;x3=x1*rann(n,1);
y=x*x2+x3;
print("x",x,"beta",x2,"epsilon",x3);
print("y",y);
print("x has ",rows(x)," rows and ",
columns(x)," columns\n");}
```

Later on (in §4.11) we shall introduce a system of name decoration, which will increase the readability of a computer program. For example, we would prefix all global variables with g_, such as g_dMisval (but we shall do our best to avoid global variables as much as possible).

2.7 Matrix constants

The previous code used various types of constants: 4 is an integer constant, 0.25 is a double constant, and "x" is a string constant. Most interesting is the value assigned to beta, which is a *matrix constant*. This is a list of numbers inside < and >, where a comma separates elements within a row, and a semicolon separates rows. The comma is actually optional. Remember that you can only use numbers in a matrix constant, no variables: <1,2,sigma> is illegal. In that case use 1~2~sigma (see§3.3).

▶[2.5] Write a program which assignes the following constants to variables, and prints the results:

```
<1,2,3>
<11 12 13; 21 22 23; 31 32 33>
<1:6>
```

2.8 Using functions

The function is a fundamental building block when writing Ox programs. Functions allow for splitting complex tasks up in manageable bits. The best ones are those which only interact with the outside via the arguments (the inputs) and the return value (the outputs, if any). Then, when there are no external variables used inside the function, the function can be treated as an isolated piece of code: the only thing which matters is the documentation of the function.

Up to this point, only one function has been used, the main function. Execution of an Ox program starts at main, from which other functions are called; there is no action outside functions. Ox comes with a vast library of functions for your convenience. These are all documented in the help and the Ox book. Whether a function is written in C, and added to the Ox system (as for the standard library), or written in Ox itself (such as the maximization functions and the Database class), does not make any difference to the user of the function.

2.8.1 Simple functions

The most simple Ox function has no arguments, and returns no value. The syntax is:

function_name ( )
{
    statements
}

For example:

```
.........................................................

#include <oxstd.h>

sometext()
{
    print("Some text\n");
}

main()
{
    sometext();
}
.........................................................
```

We've created the `sometext` function, and call it from the `main` function. When the program is run, it just prints `Some text`. Note that, to call the function, the empty parentheses are required.

2.8.2 Function arguments

A function can take arguments. In the header of the function code, the arguments are listed, separated by comma's. This example takes one argument:

```
.............................................................. oxtut2d
#include <oxstd.h>

dimensions(const mX)
{
    print("the argument has ", rows(mX), " rows", "\n");
}

main()
{
    dimensions( zeros(40, 5) );
}
..............................................................
```

The `const` which precedes each argument indicates the function is only accessing the value, not changing it. Although any change made to `mY` or `mX` is only local to the function (once the function returns, both will have their old values back), it is very useful to use `const` wherever possible: the compiler can then generate much faster code.

▶[2.6] Modify the `dimensions` function to give it two arguments, printing the number of rows in both arguments.

2.8.3 Returning a value

The return statement returns a value from the function, *and also exits the function*. So, when the program flow reaches a `return` statement, control returns to the caller, without executing the remainder of the function. The syntax of the return statement is:

> `return` *return_value* ;

Or, to exit from a function which does not have a return value:

> `return;`

For example:

```
..............................................................
MyOls1(const mY, const mX)
{
    return (mX'mX)^-1 * (mX'mY);
}
..............................................................
```

Or, using the library function `olsc`:

.... *oxtut2e*

```
#include <oxstd.h>

MyOls(const mY, const mX)
{
    decl b;

    olsc(mY, mX, &b);
    print("in MyOls(): b=", b);
    return b;
}

main()
{
    decl b;
                // mY argument, mX argument, both just random
    b = MyOls( rann(10, 1), ranu(10, 2) );
    // b now holds the result
    print("in main(): b=", b);
}
```
....

This function estimates and prints the coefficients of the linear regression model. The dependent variable is in the $n \times 1$ vector mY, and the regressors in the $n \times k$ matrix mX. The &b part is explained below. Any local variable (here: b) must be declared; b only exists while the function is active. With `return` the result is returned to the caller, and the function exited

▶[2.7] In `MyOls`, move the line with the return statement to above the print statement and compare the output with the old version.

▶[2.8] Test the function using the program given underneath: the task is to use My-Ols() for the regression. The data are observations on the weight of chickens (*y*) versus the amount of feed they were given (*X*). The data source is Judge, Hill, Griffiths, Lütkepohl and Lee (1988, Table 5.3, p.195).

.... *oxtut2f*

```
#include <oxstd.h>

MyOls(const mY, const mX)
{
    decl b;

    olsc(mY, mX, &b);
    return b;
}
main()
{
    decl y   = <0.58; 1.1; 1.2;  1.3;  1.95;
                2.55; 2.6; 2.9;  3.45; 3.5;
                3.6;  4.1; 4.35; 4.4;  4.5>;
```

```
    decl x1 = <1 : 15>';      // note transpose!
    decl mx;

    mx = 1 ~ x1 ~ x1 .^ 2;  // regressors
    print(y ~ mx);            // print all data

    // 2do: use MyOls to regress y on mx and print results
}
```

2.8.4 Function declaration

A function can only be called when the compiler knows about it. In the program listed below [2.8], the MyOls() function can be used inside main, because the source code is already known at that stage. If MyOls() were to be moved below main it cannot be used any more: the compiler hasn't yet encountered MyOls(). However, there is a way to inform about the existence of MyOls(), without yet giving the source code, namely by declaring the function. This amounts to copying the header only, terminated with a semicolon. To illustrate the principle:

```
#include <oxstd.h>

MyOls(const mY, const mX);// forward declaration of MyOls,
                          // so that it can be used in main
main()
{
    // now MyOls may be used here
}

MyOls(const mY, const mX)
{
    // code of MyOls
}
```

The header files (e.g. oxstd.h) mainly list all the function declarations together, whereas the source code resides elsewhere.

An option for small bits of code is to write the function to an .ox file, and just include the whole file into the source file which needs it.

▶[2.9] Add documentation to MyOls, using the template provided in §2.2. Save the resulting code (comment plus MyOls) in a file called myols.ox. Then adjust your program resulting from [2.8] along these lines:

```
#include <oxstd.h>

#include "myols.ox"      // insert code from myols.ox file
```

```
main()
{
    // now MyOls may be used here
}
```
....

2.8.5 Returning values in an argument

Often, a function needs to return more than one value. It was pointed out before that a function cannot make a permanent change to an argument. However, this can be changed using the ampersand (&). The following program illustrates the principle.

.... *oxtut2g*

```
#include <oxstd.h>

test1(x)        // no const, because x will be changed
{
    x = 1;
    print("in test1: ", x, "\n");
}
test2(const ax)
{
    // Note: indexing starts at 0 in Ox
    ax[0] = 2;
    print("in test2: ", ax[0], "\n");
}
main()
{
    decl x = 10;

    print("x - ", x, "\n");
    test1(x);                   // pass x
    print("x = ", x, "\n");
    test2(&x);                  // pass address of x
    print("x = ", x, "\n");
}
```
....

The program prints:
```
x = 10
in test1: 1
x = 10
in test2: 2
x = 2
```

This is happening:

- When calling test2, it receives in &x the *address* of the variable x, not its contents. In other words, we are now working with a reference to x, rather than directly with x.
- Inside test2, the ax argument holds this address. To access the contents at that

address, we use subscript 0: ax[0] is the contents of the address, which we can now change.

- ax[0] = 2 does precisely that: it changes x itself, because x resides at that address.

Consider the variable as a mailbox: a location at which a value can be stored. If the mailbox can be seen, a value can be put directly in the mailbox. Otherwise (in a function), we supply the address of the mailbox, and something can be posted to the address, also ending up in the box.

▶[2.10] Modify MyOls to print the following information:

```
Number of observations: xx
Coefficients:
   xx
   xx
Error variance:
   xx
```

▶[2.11] Modify MyOls to compute the estimated error variance. Return this through an argument.

Finally, you may use functions in expressions, or ignore the return value altogether. For example:

```
b = MyOls(my, mx) * 2;
MyOls(my, mx);
print(MyOls(my, mx));
```

Chapter 3

Operators

3.1 Introduction

A language like Ox needs at least three kinds of operators to work with matrices:

(1) index operators, to access elements in a matrix;

(2) matrix operators, for standard matrix operations such as matrix multiplication, etc.

(3) dot operators, for element by element operations.

Below, a number of matrices is created to investigate the various operators.

```
..................................................... oxtut3a
#include <oxstd.h>

main()
{
    decl im, in, vr, vc, ma, mm, mi;

    im = 3;   in = 5;
    vr = 0.1 * range(0, im - 1);
    vc = range(0, in - 1)';
    ma = vr + vc;
    mm = rann(im, im);
    mi = unit(im);
    print("vr", vr, "vc", vc,
        "ma", "%4.1f", ma,
        "mm", mm, "mi", mi);
}
.....................................................
```

This example uses a form of name decoration ('v' for vector and 'm' for matrix; this is discussed in §4.11). The print format string `"%4.1f"` is explained in §7.5.

The `unit` function creates the identity matrix, in this case of dimension `im` by `im`.

Finally, `range(0,im-1)` creates a matrix with values $0, 1, \ldots, im-1$. Since we know the value of `im`, we could have written `<0:2>`. Adding a column vector to a

19

row vector works like this:

$$(\begin{array}{cc} x_0 & x_1 \end{array}) + \left(\begin{array}{c} y_0 \\ y_1 \\ y_2 \end{array} \right) = \left(\begin{array}{cc} x_0 + y_0 & x_1 + y_0 \\ x_0 + y_1 & x_1 + y_1 \\ x_0 + y_2 & x_1 + y_2 \end{array} \right).$$

▶[3.1] Try to derive the expected output from this program on paper, then check by running it. Consult the help if necessary.

3.2 Index operators

Indexing in Ox starts at zero, not at one!

Initially you might forget this and make a few mistakes, but before too long it will become second nature. Ox has adopted this convention for compatibility with most modern languages, and because it leads to faster programs. There is an option to start at index one, which is explained in the Ox manual (and not really recommended).

A matrix usually has two indices: [i][j] indexes element (i, j) of a matrix, where [0][0] is the first (top left) element. Either i or j may be replaced by a range, such as i1:i2. If the lower value of a range is missing, zero is assumed; if the upper value is missing, the upper bound is assumed. An empty index, [] selects all rows (when it is the first index) or all columns (when it is the second).

When a matrix is used with one index, it is treated as a vector. In tht case it does not matter whether the vector is a row or a column vector. When one index is used on a proper matrix, the matrix is treated as if all the rows together make up one column vector.

Here are some examples:

$$x = \left(\begin{array}{ccc} 0 & 1 & 2 \\ 3 & 4 & 5 \end{array} \right), \quad y = (\begin{array}{ccc} 0 & 1 & 2 \end{array}), \quad z = \left(\begin{array}{c} 0 \\ 3 \\ 6 \end{array} \right).$$

$$x[0][0] = 0, \quad x[][1:] = \left(\begin{array}{cc} 1 & 2 \\ 4 & 5 \end{array} \right), \quad x[3:] = \left(\begin{array}{c} 3 \\ 4 \\ 5 \end{array} \right),$$

$$y[:1] = y[0][:1] = (\begin{array}{cc} 0 & 1 \end{array}), \quad z[:1] = z[:1][0] = \left(\begin{array}{c} 0 \\ 3 \end{array} \right).$$

▶[3.2] Write a program to verify these examples.

▶[3.3] Append the following code to the previous program. You may also wish to add additional spaces and linefeeds in the print() statements. Note: from now on we will occasionally give just a section of code; it is assumed that you know that an #include <oxstd.h> statement must be added, and the code inserted into a function (main() for example).

```
...........................................................oxtut3b
    print("vectors:",
        "vr", vr,
        "vr[0]", vr[0],
        "vr[0][0]", vr[0][0],
        "vc", vc,
        "vc[1]", vc[1],
        "vr[0][1]", vr[0][1]);
    print("matrices:",
        "ma", ma,
        "rows(ma)=", rows(ma), "columns(ma)=", columns(ma),
        "ma[1][2]", ma[1][2],
        "ma[:1][:1]", ma[:1][:1],
        "ma[][]", ma[][]);
.........................................................................
```

Finally, it is possible to use a matrix as an index. This can lead to powerful code, when combined with functions which create such indexing matrices.

▶[3.4] Again extend the program:

```
...........................................................oxtut3c
    decl rix = <1,2>, cix = <0,1>;
    print("ma", ma,
        "ma[rix][cix]", ma[rix][cix],
        "mm", mm);
    // change submatrix [rix][cix]:
    mm[rix][cix] = unit(2);
    print("mm", mm);
    // set all elements to 3:
    mm[][] - 3;
    print("mm", mm);
.........................................................................
```

The matrix indexing `ma[rix][cix]` in the previous example can be visualized as:

$$
\begin{pmatrix}
 & \downarrow & \downarrow & & & \\
 & a_{00} & a_{01} & a_{02} & a_{03} & a_{04} \\
\rightarrow & \mathbf{a_{10}} & \mathbf{a_{11}} & a_{12} & a_{13} & a_{14} \\
\rightarrow & \mathbf{a_{20}} & \mathbf{a_{21}} & a_{22} & a_{23} & a_{24}
\end{pmatrix}.
$$

3.3 Matrix operators

All operators + - * / work as expected when both operands are an integer or a double: when both operands are an integer, the result is an integer, otherwise it will be a double. The exception is division of two integers: this will produce a double, so $1/2$ equals 0.5 (C and C++ programmers take note!).

When matrices are involved, things get more interesting. Obviously, when two matrices have the same size we can add them element by element (+), or subtract them element by element ($-$). The first example of this chapter also had the 'tabular' form: adding a row vector to a column vector, producing a matrix. For matrix multiplication use $*$, then element i, j of the result is the inner product of row i (left operand) and column j (right operand).

▶[3.5] If you're not so familiar with matrices, try

$$\begin{pmatrix} 1 & 2 \\ 3 & 4 \end{pmatrix} \times \begin{pmatrix} 2 & 1 \\ 1 & 2 \end{pmatrix}$$

first on paper, then using the computer.

Division ($/$), when the right operand is a matrix, corresponds to post multiplication with the inverse. We've already used matrix transpose ($'$) and horizontal concatenation ($\tilde{}$). We also saw one useful feature when creating the constant term for regression: when concatenating an integer (or double) and a matrix, the scalar is automatically replicated to get the same number of rows ($\tilde{}$) or columns ($|$). When concatenating two non-matching matrices, the shortest one is padded with zeros at the end. (So there is a difference between 1 ˜ <1;1> and <1> ˜ <1;1> ; a warning is printed for the latter.)

A square matrix may be raised to an integer power, using ^, for example A^2 equals A*A. To summarize:

operator	operation
$'$	transpose, X'y is short for X'*y
^	(matrix) power
*	(matrix) multiplication
/	(matrix) division
+	addition
$-$	subtraction
˜	horizontal concatenation
		vertical concatenation

Some operations are illegal, resulting in an error message. Here is an example:

```
Runtime error: 'matrix[5][1] * matrix[5][3]' bad operand
Runtime error occurred in main(42), call trace:
main(42)
```

The first says that we cannot multiply a 5 × 1 matrix into a 5 × 3 matrix. The error occurred in the main function, at line 42.

▶[3.6] Return to the first example, and try all combinations of operands and operators (bearing in mind that some are not allowed). Here is a start:

```
...........................................................
print("vr",                vr);
print("vr + vr",           vr + vr);
print("ma[:2][] + mm",     ma[:2][] + mm);
print("ma * vr'",          ma * vr');
print("vc' * ma",          vc'ma);
...........................................................
```

▶[3.7] Write a program to try the following example.

```
.........................................................oxtut3d
/* a linear model */
decl ct, mx, vbeta, veps, vy;
ct = 4;
mx = 1 ~ ranu(ct, 1);
vbeta = <1;1>;
veps = 0.1 * rann(ct, 1);
vy = mx * vbeta + veps;
print("y = X * beta + eps\n",
    "X", mx, "beta", vbeta, "eps", veps, "y", vy,
    "b_hat", (1/(mx'mx)) * (mx'vy) );
...........................................................
```

This example produces the following output:

```
y = X * beta + eps
X
          1.0000        0.020192
          1.0000        0.68617
          1.0000        0.15174
          1.0000        0.74598
beta
          1.0000
          1.0000
eps
        -0.039088
        -0.064953
        -0.065276
         0.075399
y
          0.98110
          1.6212
          1.0865
          1.8214
b_hat
          0.93849
          1.0948
```

▶[3.8] Division in Ox is closely related to inversion, extend the previous example as follows:

```
...........................................................
print("b_hat", invert(mx'mx) * (mx'vy) );
print("b_hat", (mx'mx)^-1 * (mx'vy) );
```

```
print("b_hat", invertsym(mx'mx) * (mx'vy) );
print("b_hat", (1 / mx) * vy );
print("b_hat", vy'/mx');
decl vb_hat;
olsc(vy, mx, &vb_hat);// olsc,olsr are best way to do OLS!
print("b_hat", vb_hat);
```

3.4 Dot operators

Dot operators are element-by-element operators. For adding and subtracting matrices there is only the dot version, already used in the previous section (written as + and −).

Element-by-element multiplication is denoted by .* and ./ is used for element-by-element division. As with addition and subtraction, dot conformity implies that either operand may be a row (or column) vector. This is then swept through the rows (columns) of the other operand. For example:

$$
\begin{pmatrix} x_0 & x_1 \end{pmatrix} .* \begin{pmatrix} y_0 & y_1 \\ y_2 & y_3 \\ y_4 & y_5 \end{pmatrix} = \begin{pmatrix} x_0 y_0 & x_1 y_1 \\ x_0 y_2 & x_1 y_3 \\ x_0 y_4 & x_1 y_5 \end{pmatrix}.
$$

To summarize:

operator	operation
.^	element-by-element power
.*	element-by-element multiplication
./	element-by-element division
+	addition
−	subtraction

▶[3.9] Try the new operators; to start:

```
print("ma*vr'",    ma * vr');
print("ma.*vr",    ma .* vr);
print("vc'ma",     vc'ma);
print("vc .* ma",  vc .* ma);
```

▶[3.10] Adjust the linear model in [3.7] to use a matrix ϵ instead of a vector.

3.5 Relational and equality operators

Relational operators compare both operands, and exist in two versions. the first version always returns an integer, even when both arguments are matrices. The return value 0 stands for FALSE, and 1 for TRUE. When comparing a matrix to a scalar, the result is only 1 (TRUE) if it holds for each element of the matrix.

operator	operation
<	less than
>	greater than
<=	less than or equal to
=>	equal or greater than
==	is equal
! =	is not equal

The second form of relational operator is the dotted version: this does an element by element comparison, and returns a *matrix* of 0's and 1's. The dotted versions are:

operator	operation
. <	element-by-element less than
. >	element-by-element greater than
. <=	element-by-element less than or equal to
. =>	element-by-element equal or greater than
. ==	element-by-element is equal
. ! =	element-by-element is not equal

Often code is more readable when using the predefined constant TRUE and FALSE, instead of the numbers 1 and 0. These are defined in oxstd.h. Relational operators are especially important in conditional epressions and loops, and these are discussed in the next chapter.

3.6 Logical operators

These are closely related to the relational operators, and also have dotted and non-dotted versions:

operator	operation
&&	logical-and
||	logical-or

If an expression involves several logical operators after each other, evaluation will stop as soon as the final result is known. For example in (1 || checkval(x)) the function checkval is never called, because the result will be true regardless of its outcome. This is called a *boolean shortcut*.

The dotted versions are:

operator	operation
.&&	element-by-element logical-and
.||	element-by-element logical-or

The dotted operators do not have boolean shortcuts.

▶[3.11] As an example, we try to print a logical table. Print format options are used to label rows and columns, for more information see §7.1.

.... *oxtut3e*
```
#include <oxstd.h>

main()
{
    decl a1 = <0,1>, a2 = <0,1>, v = <1:3>';

    print("Truth table", "%5g ",
        "%r", {"0","1"},
        "%c", {"|| 0","|| 1", "&& 0","&& 1"},
        (a1' .|| a2) ~ (a1' .&& a2) );

    print("Some comparisons: ",
        "v ~ (v .> 1 .&& v .< 3) = ",
        v ~ (v .> 1 .&& v .< 3),
        "No dots:",
        "v ~ (v > 1 && v < 3) = ", v ~ (v > 1 && v < 3),
        " v == <1:3>' = ", v == <1:3>'
        );
}
```
....

Which prints the table:
```
Truth table
    || 0  || 1  && 0  && 1
0    0     1     0     0
1    1     1     0     1
Some comparisons: v ~ (v .> 1 .&& v .< 3) =
        1.0000        0.00000
        2.0000        1.0000
        3.0000        0.00000
No dots: v ~ (v > 1 && v < 3) =
        1.0000        0.00000
        2.0000        0.00000
        3.0000        0.00000
    v == <1:3>' = 1
```

Some procedures are available for selecting or dropping rows/columns based on a logical decision. These are `selectifr`, `selectifc`, `deleteifr` and `deleteifc`; `vecindex` may be used to translate the 0-1's to indices. A very useful, but slightly more complex operator is the dot-conditional operator (see §3.8).

Here are some examples using these functions:

`u`	1	0	1	0	2
`u .> 0`	1	0	1	0	1
`vecindex(u)'`	0	2	4		
`vecindex(u .> 1)'`	4				
`selectifc(u, u .> 0)`	1	1	2		
`selectifc(u, u .> 1)`	2				

3.7 Assignment operators

It may surprise you, but assignment is an operator like any other, it just has very low precedence (only one operator is below it: the comma operator). As a result we may write

```
decl x1, x2, x3, x4;
x1 = 0; x2 = 0; x3 = 0; x4 = 0;
// or more concisely:
x1 = x2 = x3 = x4 = 0;
```

There are also compact assignment-and-other-operation-in-one operators, for example you could try adding print statements for:

```
decl x1, x2, x3, x4;
x1 - x2 - x3 = x4 = 0;

x1 += 2;
x2 -= x1;
x1 *= 4;
x1 /= 4;
x1 ~= x2;
x3 |= 2;
```

3.8 Conditional operators

Both the conditional, and dot-conditional operators are a bit more advanced, becuase they have three components. The dot-conditional can be especially useful, because it is like a filter: a zero in the filter will not let anything through, whereas a non-zero will. Consider for example:

```
decl x = rann(2,2);
x = x .< 0 .? 0 .: x;
```

Initially, x is a matrix with standard normal random numbers. The next line checks for negative elements (x .< 0 creates a 0-1 matrix, with 1 in the positions of negative numbers). For all positions where the filter is not 0, the expression after the . ? is used. For the zeros, the else expression (after . :) is applied.

▶[3.12] Below is an example using the selectifc and vecindex functions. Adjust it to use the dot-conditional operator (use the help if necessary, see under conditional operator), to set all negative values of u to zero. Note that dot operators tend to be much faster than using loops.

. . . .*oxtut3f*

```
#include <oxstd.h>

main()
{
    decl u = rann(6,1), v, w;

    v = selectifr(u, u .< 0)';
    print(u', v');

    w = u;
    w[vecindex(u .< 0)][] = 0;
    print(u ~ w ~ vecindex(u .< 0));
}
```
. . . .

3.9 And more operators

We have not discussed all operators, see the Ox book for the full list. Some will be needed in the remaining chapters:

```
. . . . . . . . . . . . . . . . . . . . . . . . . . . . . . . . . . . . . . . . . . . . . . . . . . . . . . . . . . . .
decl x1, x2;
x1 = x2 = 0;

print(x1, " ", ++x1, "\n");            // increment x1 by 1
print(x1, " ", --x1, "\n");            // decrement x1 by 1
x1 = <0,1,2>;
print(x1, " ", !x1, " ", !!x1, "\n"); // ! is negation:
                           // 0 becomes 1, non-zero becomes 0
. . . . . . . . . . . . . . . . . . . . . . . . . . . . . . . . . . . . . . . . . . . . . . . . . . . . . . . . . . . .
```

3.10 Operator precedence

Because operator precedence is so important, we replicate the table from the Ox book here. Table 3.1 gives a summary if the operators available in Ox, together with their precedence. The precedence is in decreasing order. Operators on the same line have the same precedence, in which case the associativity gives the order of the operators.

Table 3.1   Ox operator precedence.

Category	operators	associativity
primary	`() ::`	left to right
postfix	`-> . () [] ++ -- '`	left to right
unary	`++ -- + - ! & new delete`	right to left
power	`^ .^`	left to right
multiplicative	`** * .* / ./`	left to right
additive	`+ -`	left to right
horizontal concatenation	`~`	left to right
vertical concatenation	`|`	left to right
relational	`< > <= >= .< .> .<= .>=`	left to right
equality	`== != .== .!=`	left to right
logical dot-and	`.&&`	left to right
logical-and	`&&`	left to right
logical dot-or	`.||`	left to right
logical-or	`||`	left to right
conditional	`? : .? .:`	right to left
assignment	`= *= /= += -= ~= |=`	right to left
comma	`,`	left to right

At first, it will be useful to keep Table 3.1 close at hand: we often use the precedence ordering in our statements to avoid using too many parentheses. But when in doubt, or when needing to override the default, you can always add parenthesis. For example, in [2.8] we wrote:

```
mx = 1 ~ x1 ~ x1 .^ 2;   // regressors
```

Using the precedence table we know that dot-power comes before concatenation. Also, concatenation is evaluated left to right. So the expression is evaluated as:

```
mx = ((1 ~ x1) ~ (x1 .^ 2));
```

Writing

```
mx = (1 ~ x1 ~ x1) .^ 2;
```

would have given some problems in the regression.

Chapter 4

Program Flow and Program Design

4.1 Introduction

Ox is a complete programming language, with `if` statements and `for` loops. However, where you need loops in more traditional languages, you can often use the special matrix statements available in Ox. Try to avoid loops whenever you can: the vectorized version will often be very much faster than using loops. On the other hand, you'll discover that loops cannot be avoided altogether: some code just doesn't vectorize (or the resulting code might get too complex to maintain).

4.2 `for` loops

The authors of the C language came up with a nice solution for the syntax of the for loop: it is flexible, yet readable:

```
for  ( initialization ; condition ; incrementation )
{
        statements
}
```

For example:

```
.............................................................
decl i;

for (i = 0; i < 4; ++i)
{
    print(" ", i);
}
.............................................................
```

Printing: 0 1 2 3.

It works as follows:

	value of i	check condition	action
initialize i	0	TRUE → go on	print 0
increment i	1	TRUE → go on	print 1
increment i	2	TRUE → go on	print 2
increment i	3	TRUE → go on	print 3
increment i	4	FALSE → stop!	

So, at the end of the loop, i will have the value 4. Since the condition is checked prior to executing the loop, it is possible that the body is not executed at all (then i will have the initial value).

▶[4.1] Write a function which multiplies two matrices using for loops. Compare the results with using the matrix multiplication operator.

It is allowed to have more than one statement in the initialization or incrementation part of the for loop. A comma is then required as a separator:

```
decl i, j;

for (i = 0, j = -1; i < 4 && j <= 3; ++i, j += 2)
{
    print(" ", i, " ", j);
}
```

▶[4.2] Can you see what is wrong with this code?

```
for (i = 4; i >= 0; ++i)
{
    print(" ", i);
}
```

4.3 `while` **loops**

The first example for the for loop can also be written using a while loop:

```
i = 0;
while (i < 4)
{
    print(" ", i);
    ++i;
}
```

In this case, the for loop is more readable. But if there is not a clear initialization or incrementation part, the while form might be preferred.

Again, the `while` loop is not executed at all when i starts at 4 or above. If a loop must be executed at least once, use the `do while` loop:

```
i = 0;
do
{
    print(" ", i);
    ++i;
} while (i < 4);
```

Here the check is at the end: the body is executed the first time, regardless of the initial value of i.

4.4 break **and** continue

Two special commands are available inside loops:

- `break;`
  Terminates the loop in which the command appears, for example:

  ```
  for (i = 0; i < 4; ++i)
  {
      if (i == 2) break;
      print(" ", i);
  }
  ```

Works as follows:

	i	check condition	action
initialize i	0	TRUE → go on	no break, print 0
increment i	1	TRUE → go on	no break, print 1
increment i	2	TRUE → go on	break!

- `continue;`
  Starts with the next iteration of the loop, for example:

  ```
  for (i = 0; i < 4; ++i)
  {
      if (i == 2) continue;
      print(" ", i);
  }
  ```

Works as follows:

	i	check condition	action
initialize i	0	TRUE → go on	no continue, print 0
increment i	1	TRUE → go on	no continue, print 1
increment i	2	TRUE → go on	continue!
increment i	3	TRUE → go on	no continue, print 3
increment i	4	FALSE → stop!	

4.5 Conditional statements

In the previous section we used `if` statements to illustrate the use of `continue` and `break`. The full syntax is:

```
if ( condition )
{
      statements
}
else if ( condition )
{
      statements
}
else
{
      statements
}
```

here, condition must be an expression. Remember that any non-zero value is true, and zero is FALSE. Also: a matrix is only true if it has no zero elements at all. At might seem a bit pedantic to write true in lower case, and FALSE in uppercase (and a different font). There is, however, a big difference here between true and TRUE. The latter is a predefined constant which always has the value 1 (equal to `!FALSE`). The former refers to any non-zero value, e.g. $1, 2, -12.5$, etc.

4.6 Vectorization

The following program draws T (set in the variable `ct`) normally distributed random numbers, and computes the mean of the positive numbers:

```
.......................................................... oxtut4a
#include <oxstd.h>

main()
{
    decl ct, mx, i, cpos, dsum, time;
```

```
ct = 250;
mx = rann(ct, 1);
time = timer();      // save starting time

for (i = cpos = 0, dsum = 0.0; i < ct; ++i)
{
    if (mx[i] > 0)
    {
        dsum += mx[i];
        ++cpos;
    }
}
println("lapsed time: ", timespan(time));
println("count of pos.nos: ", cpos, " out of ", ct);
println("mean of pos.nos:  ", dsum / cpos);
}
```

▶[4.3] In exercise [3.12], we used the selectifr function to select part of a matrix, based on a boolean condition. Use this knowledge to rewrite the program without using loops or conditional statements.

▶[4.4] Repeat both programs for $T = 2000, 8000$ and compare the time of the original and your vectorized program. (You might have to increase T further to get meaningful timings.)

4.7 Functions as arguments

A function may be passed as argument to another function, and then called from within that function. To pass a function as argument, just pass the name (without parentheses). The argument is then used as any other function, but there can be no argument checking at compile time, only at run time.

The examples in this section involve maximization of a function of several parameters. Fortunately, maximization code is provided with Ox, and we shall use that to illustrate using functions as arguments. The methods available in Ox are the BFGS (Broyden-Fletcher-Goldfarb-Shanno method), and the Nelder-Mead simplex method (not to be confused with the simplex method used in linear programming). Technical information on the used functions (MaxBFGS and MaxSimplex) is in the Ox manual. Details of the procedures are beyond our current objectives, but there is a vast literature on non-linear optimization techniques to consult (see, among many others, Fletcher, 1987, Gill, Murray and Wright, 1981, Cramer, 1986, Press, Flannery, Teukolsky and Vetterling, 1988, and Thisted, 1988). Note that many texts on optimization focus on minimization, rather than maximization, but of course that is just a matter of reversing the sign.

Consider minimizing the so-called Rosenbrock function:

$$f(\alpha, \beta) = 100 * \left(\beta - \alpha^2\right)^2 + (1 - \alpha)^2.$$

The minimum is at $(1, 1)$ with function value 0; the contours of the function are rather banana-shaped.

In order to use a function for maximization, it must have four arguments:

`func(const vP, const adFunc, const avScore, const amHess)`

obeying the following rules:

- vP is a $p \times 1$ matrix of parameter values at which the function is to be evaluated.
- adFunc must be the address of a variable on input. On output, the function value at the supplied parameters should be stored at the address.
- avScore holds either 0 on input, or the address of the score variable. If it was not 0 on input, the first derivatives of the function (the scores, a $p \times 1$ vector) should be stored at the address.
- We ignore the amHess argument.
- func should return 0 if it couldn't evaluate the function at the supplied parameter values, and 1 otherwise.

The initial program is:

```
.............................................................. oxtut4b
#include <oxstd.h>

fRosenbrock(const vP, const adFunc, const avScore,
    const amHess)
{
    adFunc[0] = -100 * (vP[1]  - vP[0] .^ 2) .^ 2
        - (1 - vP[0]) .^ 2;                  // function value

    return 1;                                 // 1 indicates success
}

main()
{
    decl vp, dfunc, ir;

    vp = zeros(2, 1);                         // starting values
    ir = fRosenbrock(vp, &dfunc, 0, 0);       // evaluate

    print(" function value is ", dfunc,
        "\n at parameter value:", vp');
}
.............................................................
```

▶[4.5] Below is a function which can be used to test fRosenbrock. Add it to the previous program, rewriting main to use funceval.

```
.......................................................... oxtut4c
funceval(const func, const vP)
{
    decl dfunc, ir;

    ir = func(vP, &dfunc, 0, 0);            // evaluate
    if (ir == 0)
        print("function evaluation failed\n");
    else
        print("function value is ", dfunc,
            "\n at parameter value:", vP');
}
..........................................................
```

It is a small step from here to maximize the function using MaxBFGS. When calling MaxBFGS, a function has to be provided for maximization, and MaxBFGS uses a syntax identical to that of fRosenbrock (which explains all the seemingly redundant arguments).

In addition to calling MaxBFGS (the help explains the arguments), the maximize.h header file must be included, and the object code for maximization linked in. The resulting program is:

```
.......................................................... oxtut4d
#include <oxstd.h>
#import <maximize>

fRosenbrock(const vP, const adFunc, const avScore,
    const amHess)
{
    adFunc[0] = -100 * (vP[1] - vP[0] ^ 2) ^ 2
        - (1 - vP[0]) ^ 2;                  // function value

    return 1;                               // 1 indicates success
}

main()
{
    decl vp, dfunc, ir;

    vp = zeros(2, 1);                       // starting values

    MaxBFGS(fRosenbrock, &vp, &dfunc, 0, TRUE);

    print(" function value is ", dfunc,
        "\n at parameter value:", vp');
}
..........................................................
```

▶[4.6] Use the help or documentation to read about the MaxBFGS function. Add a call to MaxControl(-1, 1); to the program in order to print the results of each iteration. Also try to inspect the return value of `MaxBFGS`: function maximization can fail for various reasons (tip: use `MaxConvergenceMsg()`).

4.8 Importing code

The previous program used the `#import` statement to incorporate the maximization code:

```
#include <oxstd.h>
#import <maximize>
```

There is no file extension in the argument to `#import`. The effect is as an `#include <maximize.h>` statement followed by marking `maximize.oxo` for linking. The actual linking only happens when the file is run, and `#import <maximize>` statements may occur in other files which need it (including compiled files).

The maximization code as supplied with Ox has three parts:

`ox/include/maximize.h`	the header file
`ox/include/maximize.oxo`	the compiled source code file
`ox/src/maximize.ox`	the original source code file

Because we link the compiled code, the original Ox code is not really needed. Program organization is discussed further in §4.10.

4.9 Global variables

A golden rule of programming is to *avoid global variables as much as possible*. The reason for this is that using global variables makes programs hard to maintain, and difficult to use. A global variable (also called *external* variable) which is only used in one source file is not too bad, but it becomes more problematic as soon as the global variables have to be shared between various source code files.

Sometimes you cannot avoid the use of global variables. In that case we recommend to label them `static` whenever possible. This will indicate that the variable can only be seen within the current file (i.e. the *scope* is restricted to the file). For example, if a procedure like `fRosenbrock` above needs to access data, we cannot avoid a global variable: the data cannot be provided as an argument, because that will stop us from using the function as an argument to `MaxBFGS`.

Another solution to the problems caused by global variables is to wrap everything into a *class*. This is the subject of Chapter 9.

To illustrate the issue, we can estimate the parameters from a normal density given a sample of size n. The normal density is:

$$f(x_i; \mu, \sigma^2) = \left(2\pi\sigma^2\right)^{-1/2} \exp\left[-\left(x_i - \mu\right)^2 / 2\sigma^2\right].$$

The log-likelihood (divided by n) for the sample is:

$$\ell(\theta|x)/n = \frac{1}{n} \sum_{i=1}^{n} \log f(x_i; \theta) = -\frac{1}{2} \log \left(2\pi\sigma^2\right) - \frac{1}{2n} \sum_{i=1}^{n} (x_i - \mu)^2 /\sigma^2.$$

Maximizing the log-likelihood amounts to doing a regression on a constant term (but in regression the estimated variance is be divided by $n - k$). So, an explicit solution is available, and code has only an illustrative purpose.

The maximand is the log-likelihood divided by the sample size, instead of just the log-likelihood. The reason for this is the convergence decision by MaxBFGS. This is based on two criteria: relative change in parameters and likelihood elasticities (parameter times score). While both are invariant to scaling of parameters, the latter is not invariant to sample size. In least squares terminology this amounts to maximizing (minus the) the residual variance, rather than the residual sum of squares.

.... *oxtut4e*

```
#include <oxstd.h>
#include <oxfloat.h>   // defines M_PI, M_2PI
#import <maximize>

static decl s_mY;       // the data sample (T x 1)
// use static to avoid any other file from seeing s_mY

fLoglik(const vP, const adFunc, const avScore,const amHess)
{
    decl dsum, dsig2;

    dsum = sumsqrc(s_mY - vP[0]) / rows(s_mY);
    dsig2 = vP[1];

    adFunc[0] = -0.5 * (log(M_2PI * dsig2) + dsum / dsig2);

    return 1;               // 1 indicates success
}

main()
{
    decl cn, dmu, dsigma2, vtheta, dfunc;

    cn = 50;                // sample size
    dmu = 21;               // distribution parameter: mean
    dsigma2 = 49;           // and variance
                            // generate a sample
    s_mY = dmu + sqrt(dsigma2) * rann(cn, 1);

    vtheta = <20;49>;
    fLoglik(vtheta, &dfunc, 0, 0);       // evaluate

    print("function value is ", cn * dfunc,
        "\nat parameter value:", vtheta');
```

```
MaxControl(-1,5);
MaxBFGS(fLoglik, &vtheta, &dfunc, 0, TRUE);

print("\nConverged function value is ", cn * dfunc,
    "\nat parameter value:", vtheta');
}
```
....

▶[4.7] Execute this program to maximize the likelihood.

Note that `fLoglik` does not check for negative variances. To make the maximization more robust it is possible to take the absolute value of the variance, using `fabs`. Then negative values will give the same likelihood as positive, and the search may extend to negative values. Of course, when the optimization is done, you may have converged to a negative variance, which needs to be made positive. There still is a singularity at zero variance. To avoid this, also insert:

```
if (dsig2 == 0)
    return 0;
```

You can see what happens when starting with a negative variance.

▶[4.8] Adjust `fLoglik` so that it works on several columns of parameters at the same time (i.e. `vP` may be $2 \times s$). Now the function is not suitable anymore for `MaxBFGS`.

4.10 Program organization

To summarize program structure as seen up to this point:

- A header file communicates the declaration of functions, constants and external variables (§2.3).
- Including Ox code makes it available for use ([2.9]).
- Precompiled code can be linked in (§4.8).

For small programs it doesn't matter so much how you organize the code. It could be convenient to set some functionality aside in an .ox file (as for `MyOls.ox`), and then include it when required.

For large programs more care is needed. Usually, the project is divided in source code according to functionality (no need to create a separate file for each function). Header files then allow the declaration to be known wherever it is required. To run the program, the code must be linked in with the `main` function, either including the code, or linking in the precompiled code.

As an example, pretend that the `fLoglik` function given above is actually of any use. First create a source code file called `myloglik.ox`:

....*oxtut4f*

```
#include <oxstd.h>
#include <oxfloat.h>    // defines M_PI

static decl s_mY;       // the data sample (T x 1)
// use static to avoid any other file from seeing s_mY

SetYdata(const mY)
{
    s_mY = mY;
}
FMyLoglik(const vP, const adFunc, const avScore,
    const amHess)
{
    decl dsum, dsig2;

    dsum = sumsqrc(s_mY - vP[0]) / rows(s_mY);
    dsig2 = vP[1];

    adFunc[0] = -0.5 * (log(M_2PI * dsig2) + dsum / dsig2);

    return 1;               // 1 indicates success
}
```
....

By making s_mY static, we hide it from other source files. In order to store data in it, we provide the SetYdata function. An alternative strategy would have been to omit the static keyword, and provide direct access to the variable.

Next, a header file called myloglik.h (don't forget the semicolons after the declarations!):

....

```
SetYdata(const mY);
FMyLoglik(const vP, const adFunc, const avScore,
    const amHess);
// if g_mY is declared without static, then access from
// other files is provided by declaring it as follows
// in the header file:
// extern decl g_mY;
```
....

(1) Including the code:

....

```
#include <oxstd.h>
#include "myloglik.h"          // no <...> but "..."

#include "myloglik.ox"         // also get the code

main()
{   // main code has to be supplied
}
```
....

(2) Linking the pre-compiled code requires compilation first. You could use `oxl.exe` for example:

```
oxl -c myloglik.ox
```

This will produce `myloglik.oxo`. Then use:

```
.............................................................
#include <oxstd.h>
#import "myloglik"     // no <...> but "...", no .h

main()
{
    // main code
}
.............................................................
```

(3) An alternative way of linking the pre-compiled code is:

```
.............................................................
#include <oxstd.h>
#include "myloglik.h"            // no <...> but "..."

#pragma link("myloglik.oxo")  // link object code

// main code
.............................................................
```

This pragma may only occur once for each `.oxo` file in every program.

(4) Or, linking on the command line, assuming that the main program is called `myprog.ox`:

```
oxlw -lmyloglik myprog.ox
```

Note, that you must recreate the `myloglik.oxo` file any time you make a change in `myloglik.ox`.

▶[4.9] Try the various procedures outlined above, and compare the outcomes. Use `SetYdata` to change the contents of `m_sY`.

4.11 Style and Hungarian notation

The readability and maintainability of a program is considerably enhanced when using a consistent style and notation, together with proper indentation and documentation. Style is a personal matter; this section describes the style adopted in the Ox manual. Indent by four spaces at the next level of control (i.e. after each opening brace), jumping back on the closing brace.

The Ox manual also uses something called Hungarian notation. This involves the decoration of variable names. There are two elements to Hungarian notation: prefixing of variable names to indicate type (Table 4.2), and using case to indicate scope (Table 4.1, remember that Ox is case sensitive).

As an example consider:

```
................................................................
#include <oxstd.h>

const decl MX_R = 2;                          /* a constant */
decl g_mX;                              /* exported matrix */
static decl s_iCount;          /* static external variable */

static func1(const amX)/*argument is address of variable */
{
    amX[0] = unit(2);
}
                                      /* exported function */
Func2(const mX, const asX, const cT, const cX)
{
    decl i, my, cn;
    // etc.
}
................................................................
```

The func1 function is only used in this file, and gets the address of a variable as argument. Func2 is exported to other files, and expects a cT × cX matrix, and corresponding array of cX variable names. The c prefix is used for the number of elements in a matrix or string (c for count of). Note however, that it is not necessary in Ox to pass dimensions separately. You can ask mX and asX what dimensions they have:

```
................................................................
Func2(const mX, const asX)
{
    decl i, m, ct, cx;
    cx = columns(mX);
    ct = rows(mX);
    if (cx != sizeof(asX))
        print("error: dimensions don't match");
}
................................................................
```

Table 4.1   Hungarian notation, case sensitivity.

local variables	all lowercase
function (not exported)	first letter lowercase
function (exported)	first letter uppercase
static external variable	s_ prefix, type in lower, next letter uppercase
exported external (global) variable	as above, but prefixed with g_
function argument	type in lowercase, next letter uppercase
constants	all uppercase

Table 4.2   Hungarian notation prefixes.

prefix	type	example
i	integer	iX
c	count of	cX
b	boolean (f is also used)	bX
f	boolean (and integer flag)	fX
d	double	dX
m	matrix	mX
v	vector	vX
s	string	sX
a	array (or address)	aX
as	array of strings	asX
am	array of matrices	amX
p	pointer (function argument)	pX
m_	class member variable	m_mX
g_	external variable with global scope	g_mX
s_	static external variable (file scope)	s_mX

Chapter 5

Input and Output

5.1 Introduction

Table 5.1 lists the files types which Ox can read and write.

file type	default extension
ASCII matrix file	.mat
ASCII data file with load information	.dat
PcGive/GiveWin data file	.in7 (with .bn7)
Excel spreadsheet file	.xls
Lotus spreadsheet file	.wks/.wk1
Gauss data file	.dht (with .dat)
Gauss matrix file	.fmt
binary file using low level functions	

Table 5.1   Supported file formats.

Simple functions are available for reading and writing, as are low level functions which can be used to read virtually any binary data file (provided the format is known; see the examples in samples\inout). This chapter gives examples of the most frequently used methods, but is by no means exhaustive.

To read a file directly into a matrix, use loadmat. The loadmat function uses the extension of the file name to determine the file type. Use savemat to write a matrix to disk, again the file type is determined by the extension.

All versions of Ox, whether for Unix or Windows, will write identical files. So you can write a PcGive file on the Sun, transfer it to a PC (.in7 and binary transfer for .bn7!), and read it there.

5.2 Using paths in Ox

If you specify full folder names, you must either use one forward slash, or two back-slashes: `"./data.mat"` or `".\\data.mat"`. Ox will interpret one backslash in a string as an escape sequence (as in `"\n"`, see §7.4); only if it happens not to be an escape sequence, will the backslash be used. Also note that the Windows and Unix versions of Ox can handle long file names.

5.3 Using GiveWin or Excel

If you need to enter data from the keyboard, you can enter these into a file using a text editor, or enter them into a GiveWin database or Excel spreadsheet. These can be read directly into an Ox matrix or into an Ox database. Examples are given below.

5.4 Matrix file (.mat)

This is a simple ASCII (human-readable) file. The first two numbers in the file give the number of rows and columns of the matrix, this is followed by the matrix elements, row by row. If `data.mat` has the following contents:

```
4 2   // 4 by 2 matrix

1 2   // comment is allowed
3 4
5 6   7 8
```

then the following program will read it, provided it is in the same directory.

```
#include <oxstd.h>

main()
{
    decl mx;

    mx = loadmat("data.mat");

    print(mx);
}
```

▶[5.1] Rewrite [2.8] by putting the data in a .mat file. To save typing the numbers, you can first run the program with a `savemat` command.

5.5 Spreadsheet files

Ox can read and write the following spreadsheet files:

- Excel: .xls files;
- Lotus: .wks, .wk1 files;

provided the following convention is adopted:

- Ordered by observation (that is, variables are in columns).
- Columns with variables are labelled (have a name).
- There is an unlabelled column with the dates (as a string), in the form year–period (the – can actually be any single character), for example, 1980–1 (or: 1980Q1 1980P1 1980:1 etc.). This doesn't have to be the first column.
- The data form a contiguous sample (non-numeric fields are converted to missing values, so you can leave gaps for missing observations). Here –9999.99 is used as the missing value.

Ox can read the following types of Excel files:

- Excel 2.1, 3.0, 4.0 worksheets;
- Excel 5.0, 95, 97 workbooks.

Workbooks are compound files, and only the first sheet in the file is read. If Ox cannot read a workbook file, it is recommended to retry with a worksheet file.

When saving a database as an Excel file, it is written as an Excel 2.1 worksheet. The maximum size of spreadsheet files is 65 536 rows by 256 columns, and a warning is given if that maximum is exceeded (Ox can handle much larger datasets). Ox does not enforce the maximum number of columns, allowing up to 65 536 instead; rows and columns in excess of 65 536 are not written.

For example, the format for writing is (this is also the optimal format for reading):

	A	B	C	D
1		CONS	INFL	DUM
2	1980-1	883	2.7	3
3	1980-2	884	3.5	5
4	1980-3	885	3.9	1
5	1980-4	889	2.6	9
6	1981-1	900	3.4	2

5.6 GiveWin/PcGive data files (.IN7/.BN7)

As for spreadsheet and matrix files, these can be read directly into a matrix using the `loadmat` function.

▶[5.2] Adjust the program you wrote in §5.4 to save the matrix file in the PcGive file format. If you have access to GiveWin, then load the file into it. Or, if you have access to Excel, you can try to use the spreadsheet format instead.

5.7 What about variable names?

Often the columns of the matrix to be read in are variables for modelling which have a name. It would be nice to have those names in the output, or even select variables by name. This functionality is offered by the *database class*. We will start later with object oriented programming, but the following example could already be useful. The database class also has facilities to keep track of time-series data.

The examples will use the `data.in7/data.bn7` file combination, installed with Ox in the `ox\samples\database` directory.

.... *oxtut5a*

```
#include <oxstd.h>
#include <database.h>
#pragma link("database.oxo")

main()
{   decl dbase;

    dbase = new Database();
    dbase->LoadIn7(
        "C:/Program files/Ox/Data/data.in7");

    dbase->Info();

    delete dbase;
}
```
....

With output:

```
---- Database information ----

4 variables, 159 observations

name          sample period       min     mean     max  stddev
CONS       1953 (1) 1992 (3)     853.5   875.94  896.83  13.497
INC        1953 (1) 1992 (3)    870.22   891.69  911.38  10.725
INFLAT     1953 (1) 1992 (3)   -0.6298   1.7997  6.4976  1.2862
OUTPUT     1953 (1) 1992 (3)    1165.9   1191.1  1213.3  10.974
```

▶[5.3] Try the above program, using the correct path for your installation.

▶[5.4] With mx = dbase->GetAll(); you can get the whole database matrix into
the variable mx. Use meanc etc. to replicate the database information.

5.8 Finding that file

In the previous section we hardcoded the file name. That is not always convenient,
especially not with distributed code where it is up to the user to determine the file
locations. There are a couple of tricks which may help:

.... *oxtut5b*
```
#include <oxstd.h>
#import <database>
#import <data/>

main()
{   decl dbase;

    decl x = loadmat("data/data.in7");
    print("means:", meanc(x));

    dbase = new Database();
    dbase->LoadIn7("data.in7");
    dbase->Info();

    delete dbase;
}
```
....

If you have installed properly (i.e. the OXPATH variable is set correctly), then in
both cases the files will be found.

- loadmat works, because, when normal file opening fails, the file is searched
  along OXPATH. In this case, the file is in ox/data, so the second search succeeds.
- LoadIn7 works with the help of the import statement. The argument to import is a partial path (because of the terminating slash). That relative path is
  now combined with OXPATH to continue the search.

Chapter 6

Graphics

6.1 Introduction

We assume that you have GiveWin or can handle PostScript files, requiring:

(1) access to OxRun and GiveWin to see graphs on screen, or
(2) access to GhostView or another program to view a saved graph on screen, or
(3) access to a PostScript printer to print a saved graph, or
(4) access to a GhostScript or another program to print a saved graph.

More details follow.

6.2 Graphics output

Several types of graphs are readily produced in Ox, such as graphs over time of several variables, cross-plots, histograms, correlograms, etc. Although all graph saving will work on any system supported by Ox, only a few can display graphs on screen (GiveWin can, for example). If you have GhostView installed, you can use that to display a saved PostScript file on your screen.

A graph can be saved in various formats:

- Encapsulated PostScript (.eps),
- PostScript (.ps), and
- GiveWin graphics file (.gwg).

When using *GiveWin*, graphs can also be saved in Windows Metafile format (.wmf), and copied to the clipboard for pasting into wordprocessors.

6.3 Running programs with graphics

- Windows graphics from the console version
  Ox1 cannot display graphics, but can save graphics.

49

- Graphics from Unix console versions
  These cannot display graphics, but can save graphics.
- Windows graphics (*OxRun* and *GiveWin*)
  Text and graphics output from the Ox program will appear in *GiveWin*. There,
  text and graphs can be edited further, or copied to the clipboard for pasting into
  other programs.

6.4 Example

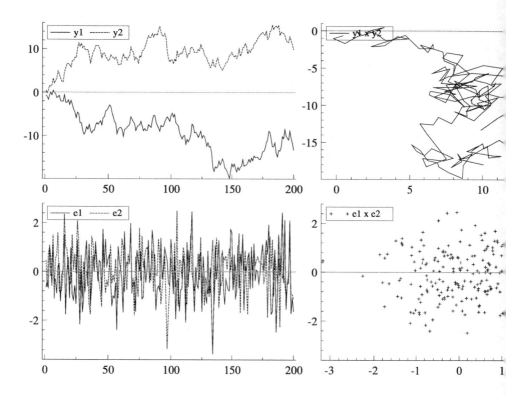

The example program generates two drawings from a standard normal distribution,
cumulates these to get two independent random walks. These are then drawn against
time (both in one graph) and against each other, resulting in two graphs.

·· *oxtut6a*

```
#include <oxstd.h>
#include <oxdraw.h>

main()
{
```

```
      decl ct = 200, meps, msum;

      meps = rann(ct, 2);
      msum = cumulate(meps);

      DrawTMatrix(0, msum', {"y1", "y2"}, 1, 1, 1);
      DrawXMatrix(1, msum[][0]', {"y1"}, msum[][1]', "y2");

      ShowDrawWindow();
}
```

The `oxdraw.h` must be included for the graphics functions. Some remarks on the functions used:

- `DrawTMatrix()` graphs variables against time. *It expects the data in rows.* The startyear(startperiod) is 1(1), with frequency 1. This gives an x-axis which is $1, 2, 3, \ldots$. The first argument is the area index, here 0 for the first plot.
- `DrawXMatrix()` graphs variables against another variable. *It expects the data in rows.* The x-axis is given by the second variable. The first argument is the area index, here 1 for the second plot.
- `ShowDrawWindow()` is required to realize the graph on screen. It also clears the drawing buffer for subsequent graphs.
- You may add a call to `SaveDrawWindow()` to save the graph to disk. The extension determines the file type: `.gwg` for GiveWin graphics, `.eps` for encapsulated `PostScript` and `.ps` for `PostScript`.

▶[6.1] The listed program only shows the first two graphs of the figure above. The additional graphs are the two standard normal drawings, and their cross plot. Add two lines to the program so that the full figure is replicated.

Chapter 7

Strings, Arrays and Print Formats

7.1 Introduction

In addition to matrices (and integers and doubles), Ox also supports strings and arrays. We have been using strings all the time to clarify the program output. An example of a *string constant* is `"some text"`. Once this string is assigned to a variable, that variable has the string type.

In [3.11] we even used an array of strings: `{"0","1"}`. This type is especially useful to label rows and/or columns of a matrix. Here is another example:

```
.................................................................... oxtut7a
#include <oxstd.h>

main()
{
    print( "%r", {"row 1", "row 2"},
           "%c", {"col 1", "col 2"}, "%6.1g", unit(2) );
}
....................................................................
```

producing:

```
        col 1 col 2
row 1     1     0
row 2     0     1
```

This program has 7 string constants, and 2 arrays. The strings which have the % symbol are *format specifiers*, to be discussed later.

7.2 String operators

Most useful are string concatenation (˜ but | will also work), and string indexing. Since a string is a one dimensional construct, it takes only one index. For example:

```
...............................................................
#include <oxstd.h>

main()
{
    decl s = "some";

    s ~= " text";
    print(s, s[4:], "\nsize of s = ", sizeof(s));
}
...............................................................
```

7.3 The sprint function

The sprint function works exactly like print, but it returns the output as a string, instead of printing it to the screen. Together with concatenation, this allows for easy creation of text in the program.

In the next example we use sprint to write intermediate results to a file, where the filename depends on the replication. This apprach might be useful during very lengthy computations, to allow inspection of results before the program is complete.

```
.......................................................... oxtut7b
#include <oxstd.h>

main()
{
    decl crep = 4, ct = 50, i, sfile, mx;

    for (i = 0; i < crep; ++i)
    {
        mx = rann(ct, 1); // some lengthy calculation
        sfile = sprint("step", i, ".mat");
        savemat(sfile, mx);
        print("Step ", i, " saved to \"", sfile,
            "\"; mean:", meanc(mx));
    }
}
...............................................................
```

▶[7.1] Run the above program, then write the counterpart. This should read in the created files, and compute the means of the data in those files.

7.4 Escape sequence

Escape sequences are special characters embedded in a string. They start with a backslash. The previous example used \ " to insert a double quote in a string. We also used \n, which inserts a newline character. Some useful ones are:

\"	double quote (")
\0	null character
\\	backslash (\)
\a	alert (bel)
\b	backspace
\n	newline
\t	horizontal tab

The most important is perhaps the backslash itself, because that is used in filenames. So write `"c:\\ox\\bin"`. You may also use forward slashes in Ox, then only one is required: `"c:/ox/bin"`.

7.5 Print formats

Without specifying an output format, all output is written in the default format. You can change both the global default output format, as well as specify a format for the next object in the `print` function.

Examples of the latter were in §7.1. There we used `"%6.1g"` to print the matrix in *general* format (which uses scientific notation if the numbers become too small or large), using an output field of 5 characters with 1 significant digit. In addition `"%r"` was used to indicate that the next argument is an array of strings to label the rows, whereas `"%c"` was used for column labels. A full description is in the online help, and in the manual.

The `format` function may be used to set the global format, for example:

```
format("%#13.5g");    // set new default format for doubles
format(200);          // increase line length to 200
```

`"%#13.5g"` is actually already the default for writing doubles such as matrix elements. The defaults will usually suffice, so perhaps it is more common to temporarily override it in the `print` function than using the `format` command.

▶[7.2] Use the following program to experiment with some formats.

```
............................................................ oxtut7c
#include <oxstd.h>

main()
{
    decl mx;

    mx = ranu(1,1) ~ ranu(1,1) / 10000;
    print("%25.16g", mx, "%25.4g", mx, "%25.4f", mx);
}
............................................................
```

7.6 Arrays

A matrix is a two-dimensional array of real numbers, and cannot contain any other data types. Arrays give more flexibility. An array is a one-dimensional array of any object. Note that this is a recursive definition: an element in an array may be an array itself, making high dimensional arrays possible.

An array is constructed from variables by the use of curly braces, or by using the `new array[`*dim*`]` statement. When an array is printed, all elements are listed. Arrays can be concatenated, and indexed. Section 7.1 showed an array of strings: `{"row 1", "row 2"}`. Here is a more elaborate example which mixes types in an array:

....*oxtut7d*

```
#include <oxstd.h>

main()
{
    decl x = unit(2), ar;

    ar = {x, {"row 1", "row 2"}, {"col 1", "col 2"} };
    print(ar);

    ar = {x, { {"row 1", "row 2"}, {"col 1", "col 2"} };
    print(ar);
}
```

....

producing:
```
[0] -
        1.0000        0.00000
        0.00000       1.0000
[1][0] = row 1
[1][1] = row 2
[2][0] = col 1
[2][1] = col 2

[0] =
        1.0000        0.00000
        0.00000       1.0000
[1][0][0] = row 1
[1][0][1] = row 2
[1][1][0] = col 1
[1][1][1] = col 2
```

7.7 Missing values

There is one type of missing value which is supported by computer hardware. It is called *Not a Number*, or NaN for short.

In a matrix constant, you may use a dot to represent a NaN. You may also use the predefined constant M_NAN (defined in `oxfloat.h`). The format used when printing output is .NaN. The spaces around the dot in the example are necessary, otherwise `.>` is interpreted as a dot-greater than:

```
#include <oxstd.h>
#include <oxfloat.h>   // defines M_NAN

main()
{
    decl m = < . >, d = M_NAN;

    print(m + 1, d / 2);
}
```

Any computation involving a NaN results in a NaN. A number of procedures are available to deal with missing values, most importantly:

- `deletec()`: deletes all columns which have a NaN,
- `deleter()`: deletes all rows which have a NaN,
- `selectc()`: selects all columns which have a NaN,
- `selectr()`: selects all rows which have a NaN,
- `isdotnan()`: returns matrix of 0's and 1's: 1 if the element is a NaN, 0 otherwise,
- `isnan()`: returns 1 if *any* element is a NaN, 0 otherwise.

`isdotnan` in combination with the dot-conditional operator is an easy way to replace missing values by another value:

```
#include <oxstd.h>

main()
{
    decl m1 = <0,.;.,1>, m2;

    m2 = isdotnan(m1) .? -10 .: m1;   // replace NaN by -10
    print(m1, m2);
}
```

7.8 Infinity

Infinity also exists as a special value supported by the hardware. Infinity can be positive or negative (printed as `+.Inf` and `-.Inf`), and can be used in comparisons as any normal number. The `isdotinf()` function tests for infinity.

►[7.3] Write a little program to experiment with NaN and infinity. Generate a NaN as the logarithm of a negative number, and infinity as the exponent of a large number. Investigate how they behave when multiplied/divided by each other or a normal number.

Chapter 8

Summary

8.1 Style

- Use interpretable names for your variables.
- Use Hungarian notation (§4.11) to indicate the type and scope of your variables.
- Use indentation and spaces to structure your programs. For example 4 spaces in (or a tab) after {, and four out for the }.
- Document your code.
- Use text to clarify your output.
- Only put more than one statement on a line if this improves readability.

8.2 Functions

- Split large projects up in several files (§4.10).
- First try each function separately on a small problem.
- Avoid the use of global (external) variables. If possible make them `static`, otherwise prefix global variables which have global scope with `g_`. Consider creating a class if you need to set many global variables.

8.3 Efficient programming

- Prepare a brief outline before you start programming.
- Use standard library functions whenever possible.
- Try to find examples which solve a related problem.
- Experiment with small problems before tackling larger ones.
- Start simulation experiments with a small number of replications. Use the `timer` and `timespan` functions to estimate the time it will take. If it is a few days or weeks, split the program in smaller parts.

8.4 Computational speed

- Use matrices as much as you can, avoiding loops and matrix indexing.
- Use the `const` argument qualifier when an argument is not changed in a function: this allows for more efficient function calling.
- Use built-in functions where possible.
- When optimizing a program with loops, it usually only pays to optimize the inner most loop. One option is to move loop invariants to a variable outside the loop.
- Avoid using 'hat' matrices (such as $X(X'X)^{-1}X'$), i.e. avoid using outer products over large dimensions when not necessary.
- If necessary, you can link in C or Fortran code, as explained in the Ox manual.

Chapter 9

Classes

9.1 Introduction

Object-oriented programming might sound rather daunting at first, but this chapter will try to show that it is not that difficult, and can be used to much benefit. Note that it is an optional feature, and powerful programs can be written without it. The syntax of object oriented programming in Ox is a subset of that in C++. This makes it similar to the approach taken in Java.

As always, there is some terminology to get used to. The main vehicle of object-oriented programming is the *class*, which is the definition of an object (somewhat like the abstract concept of a car). For it to work in practice requires creating *objects* of that class (your own car is the object: it is difficult to drive around in an abstract concept). It is with these objects that the program works.

Classes have two types of *members*: variables (the *data*) and functions (the *methods* which work on that data).

Inheritance is important here: a van can inherit (or derive) much of its functionality from a basic car. This avoids the need to start again from scratch. The same is applied in programming: a derived class inherits all the members of the base class; only the new bells and whistles need to be added.

Say we wish to implement a Monte Carlo experiment. The basic class will store the replication results, and do all the bookkeeping. To be general, we wish it to be unaware of what it is actually simulated. But how can it call a function (called Generate, say), if that function doesn't exist yet? (And it will not exist until we design the actual experiment.) This is where a *virtual* function comes into play: if a derived class has its own new version of `Generate`, the base class will automatically use that one, instead of the original version.

A *constructor* function is called when the object is created, and is used to do all necessary initializations. A constructor has the same name as the class. A *destructor* function cleans up (if necessary) when finished. A destructor has the same name as the class, but is prefixed with a ~.

9.2 Regression example

The very first example using classes was given in §5.7. Here is another example using one (actually: three!) of the preprogrammed classes:

.... *oxtut9a*

```
#include <oxstd.h>
#import <pcfiml>

main()
{
    decl model;
    model = new PcFiml();

    model.LoadIn7("data/data.in7");
        // create deterministic variables in the database
    model.Deterministic(FALSE);
                                // formulate the model
    model.Select(Y_VAR, { "CONS", 0, 1 } );  // lag 0 to 1
    model.Select(X_VAR, { "INC", 0, 1 } );    // lag 0 to 1
    model.Select(X_VAR, { "Constant", 0, 0 } );// no lags!

    model.SetSelSample(-1, 1, -1, 1);    // maximum sample
    model.Estimate();                    // estimate the model

    delete model;
}
```
....

This estimates a model by ordinary least squares:

$$y_t = \beta_0 + \beta_1 y_{t-1} + \beta_2 x_t + \beta_3 x_{t-1} + \epsilon_t,$$

where y_t is *CONS* (consumption from the artificial data set data.in7/data.bn7), x_t is *INC* (income).

The PcFiml class is for estimating linear regression models (even multivariate), with options for diagnostic testing, cointegration analysis and simultaneous equations estimation (using Full Information Maximum Likelihood estimation, hence the name). Here it is used in its simplest form.

A few points related to the program:

- The necessary .oxo files must be linked in. Here that is achieved by importing pcfiml. There are actually three linked in: maximize.oxo, database.oxo and pcfiml.oxo.
- new creates a new object of the PcFiml class, and puts it in the variable called model. Note the parentheses, just like a function call. Actually: there is a function call, namely the constructor function is called.
- Compare the data loading part with the code in §5.7. They're exactly the same! This is because PcFiml derives from the Database class, so it automatically inherits all the data input/output functionality.

- To call functions from the object, use . or ->. (We will use both in this chapter; the equivalence of . and -> was only introduced with Ox version 2.00.) From the outside there is only access to functions, not to any of the data members.
- Deterministic() creates a constant term, trend, and seasonal dummies. Again, this is Database code being used.
- Select formulates the model: Y_VAR for dependent and lagged dependent variabeles, X_VAR for the other regressors. The second argument is an array with three elements: variable name, start lag and end lag.
- SetSelSample sets the maximum sample, but could also be used to select a subsample.
- Estimate estimates and prints the results. How much work would this have been starting from scratch?
- Finally, when done, we delete the object. This calls the destructor function, and then clears the object from memory. When creating objects without calling delete afterwards, memory consumption will keep on increasing.

The output from the program is:

```
---- System estimation by OLS ----
The estimation sample is 1953 (2) 1992 (3)
CONS            lag 0 status Y
CONS            lag 1 status Y
INC             lag 0 status X
INC             lag 1 status X
Constant        lag 0 status X

coefficients
                        CONS
CONS_1               0.98587
INC                  0.49584
INC_1               -0.48491
Constant              2.5114

coefficient standard errors
                        CONS
CONS_1              0.027620
INC                 0.037971
INC_1               0.041031
Constant              11.393

equation standard errors
          CONS
        1.4800

residual covariance
                CONS
CONS          2.1903

log-likelihood=-59.9149683 det-omega=2.13489 T=158
```

▶[9.1] Run the above program. When successful, add *INFLAT* to the model (without any lags), and re-estimate. Surprised by the large change in the coefficients? Then see the chapter called Intermediate Econometrics in Hendry and Doornik (1996).

▶[9.2] Building on the knowledge of the previous chapters, replicate the coefficient estimates from the first model. Use `loadmat` to load the data in a matrix (Ch. 5), the order of the data is: *CONS, INC, INFLAT, OUTPUT*. Use `lag0` to create lagged variables, and `olsc` to do the regression.

9.3 Simulation example

The example discussed here generates data from a standard normal distribution, and estimates the mean and variance (similar to §4.9, but now using analytical solutions. It also tests whether the mean is different from zero.

The data are drawn from a normal distribution, so that the data generation process (DGP) is:

$$y_t = \mu + \epsilon_t \text{ with } \epsilon_t \sim N(0, \sigma^2).$$

We choose $\mu = 0$ and $\sigma^2 = 1$. The parameters are estimated from a sample of size T by:

$$\hat{\mu} = T^{-1} \sum_{t=0}^{T-1} y_t, \quad \hat{\sigma}^2 = T^{-1} \sum_{t=0}^{T-1} (y_t - \hat{\mu})^2,$$

and

$$\hat{s} = \left\{ (T-1)^{-1} \sum_{t=0}^{T-1} (y_t - \hat{\mu})^2 \right\}^{\frac{1}{2}} = \left\{ \frac{T}{T-1} \hat{\sigma}^2 \right\}^{\frac{1}{2}}.$$

The t-test which tests the hypothesis $H_0: \hat{\mu} = 0$ is:

$$\hat{t} = T^{\frac{1}{2}} \frac{\hat{\mu}}{\hat{s}}.$$

The properties of the estimated coefficients and test statistic are studied by repeating the experiment M times, and averaging the outcome of the M experiments. We could have done this Monte Carlo experiment analytically (which, of course, is much more accurate and also much more general). But for more complicated problems, the analytical solution often becomes intractable, and the Monte Carlo experiment is the only way to investigate the properties of tests or estimators. For more information on Monte Carlo analysis see Davidson and MacKinnon (1993, Ch. 21), Hendry (1995, Ch. 3) and Ripley (1987).

▶[9.3] Write a program which draws a sample of size 50 from the DGP and computes $\hat{\mu}$, $\hat{s}$ and $\hat{t}$. When that is working, add a loop of size M around this. We wish to store the results of the M replications to compute the average $\hat{\mu}$ and $\hat{s}$ from those M numbers. The added code could be of the form (this is incomplete):

```
. . . . . . . . . . . . . . . . . . . . . . . . . . . . . . . . . . . . . . . . . . . . . . . . . . . . . . . . . . . oxtut9b
decl cm = 1000, mresults;
mresults = zeros(3, cm); // precreate matrix

for (i = 0; i < cm; ++i)
{
    // generate results
    mresults[0][i] =  // store mean here
    mresults[1][i] =  // store std.dev. here
    mresults[2][i] =  // store t-value here
}
// compute averages of mean and std.dev
// perhaps draw histogram of t-values
. . . . . . . . . . . . . . . . . . . . . . . . . . . . . . . . . . . . . . . . . . . . . . . . . . . . . . . . . . .
```

Theory tells us that the t-values have a Student-t distribution with 49 degrees of freedom. In `mresults[2][]` we now have 1000 drawings from that distribution, and a histogram of this data should be close to a t(49) distribution. Similarly, after sorting the numbers, entry 949 should correspond to the 5% critical value which may be found in tables. This is also called the 95% quantile of the test.

▶[9.4] Add code to your program to print the 95% quantile of the simulated *t*-values. Use both the `sortr()` function and the `quantiler()` function. Also report the theoretical quantile from a t(49) distribution using `quant()`.

So much for the theory. The following program repeats the Monte Carlo experiment, based on the Simulation class, and using $T = 50$ and $M = 1000$. The new class `SimNormal` derives from the `Simulation` class. Now there seems to be a setback: the new program is more than twice as long as the not object-oriented version. Indeed, for small, simple problems there is a case for sticking with the simple code. Although: we now do get a nice report as output (without any effort), which is still missing from the simple code. And, without modifications we can run it for various sample sizes at once. In the next section, we will create our own (simpler) version of the Simula class.

▶[9.5] Run the program below. Note that when a Monte Carlo program is modified, there could be two reason for getting different results: (1) the initial seed of the random generator is different, (2) a different amount of random numbers is drawn, so after one replication they don't match anymore.

```
. . . . . . . . . . . . . . . . . . . . . . . . . . . . . . . . . . . . . . . . . . . . . . . . . . . . . . . . . . . oxtut9c
#include <oxstd.h>
#import <simula>        // import simulation header and code

/*--------------- SimNormal : Simulation ---------------*/
class SimNormal : Simulation      // inherit from simulation
{
    decl m_mCoef;                           // coefficient
    decl m_mTest;                          // test statistic
    decl m_mPval;                         // p-value of t-test
```

```
    SimNormal();                              // constructor
      // Generate() replaces the virtual function with the
   // same name of the base class to generate replications
    Generate(const iRep, const cT, const mxT);
                    //these also replace virtual functions:
    GetCoefficients();         // return coefficient values
    GetPvalues();              // return p-values of tests
    GetTestStatistics();        // return test statistics
};
SimNormal::SimNormal()                    // define constructor
{
    this->Simulation(<50>, 50, 1000, TRUE, ranseed(-1),
        <0.2,0.1,0.05,0.01>,    // p-values to investigate
        <0,1>);                 // true coefs: mean=0, sd=1
    this->SetTestNames({"t-value"});         // set names
    this->SetCoefNames({"constant", "std.dev"});
}
SimNormal::Generate(const iRep, const cT, const mxT)
{
    decl my, sdevy, meany;

    my = rann(cT, 1);                       // generate data

    meany = meanc(my);                      // mean of y
    sdevy = sqrt(cT * varc(my) / (cT-1));   // std.dev of y

    m mCoef = meany | sdevy;                // mean,sdev of y
    m_mTest = meany / (sdevy / sqrt(cT));//t-value on mean
    m_mPval = tailt(m_mTest, cT-1);  // t(T-1) distributed

return 1;
}
SimNormal::GetCoefficients()
{
    return m_mCoef;
}
SimNormal::GetPvalues()
{
    return m_mPval;
}
SimNormal::GetTestStatistics()
{
    return m_mTest;
}
/*------------ END SimNormal : Simulation --------------*/

main()
{
    decl experiment = new SimNormal();    // create object

    experiment->Simulate();                // do simulations
```

```
        delete experiment;                      // remove object
    }
    ................................................................
```

▶[9.6] We obtained the output below. Try to interpret these results.

```
T=50, M=1000, seed=198195252 (common)

test moments
                        mean     std.dev   skewness ex.kurtosis
t-value            -0.056647      1.0135  -0.012933      0.15601

critical values (tail quantiles)
                        20%         10%          5%          1%
t-value             0.80563      1.2758      1.6512      2.2456

rejection frequencies
                        20%         10%          5%          1%
t-value             0.18500    0.097000    0.049000   0.0050000

coefficient moments
                        mean     std.dev
constant          -0.0074297     0.14044
std.dev             0.99471     0.10130

coefficient biases
                  mean bias         rmse se meanbias true value
constant          -0.0074297     0.14064   0.0044412     0.00000
std.dev           -0.0052933     0.10144   0.0032035     1.0000
```

9.4 MySimula class

9.4.1 The first step

A class is declared as follows (the part in square brackets is only used when deriving from an existing class, as in the example above):

```
class class_name [: base_class]
{
        class_members
};
```

Note the semicolon at the end.

Our class starts as:

```
class MySimula
{
    MySimula();                     // constructor
};
```

Where the constructor is already *declared* as a first function member. A member function is then *defined* as

class_name : : *member_function* (*arguments*)
{
    function_body
}

Adding the definition for the constructor yields:

.... *oxtut9d*

```
#include <oxstd.h>

class MySimula
{
    MySimula();                 // constructor
};
MySimula::MySimula()
{
    print("MySimula constructor called\n");
}

main()
{
    decl mysim;

    mysim = new MySimula();

    delete mysim;
}
```
....

▶[9.7] Run the program given above.

▶[9.8] As does the constructor, the destructor has the same name as the class, but to distinguish it, it is prefixed with a ~ symbol. The destructor is called ~MySimula(). Modify the code to declare the destructor in the class. Add the destructor function and make it also print a message. No changes have to be made to main.

9.4.2 Adding data members

The main variables needed are M, T, and storage for the replicated mean and standard deviations (we concentrate on those first, calling them 'coefficients'). We use Hungarian notation (§4.11). The constructor receives values for M, T as arguments. A Simulate function is used to do the experiment, and a Report function to report the results.

You may have noted that from inside a member function, we can call other member functions without needing the arrow notation (but this-> and this. are allowed). Member variables may be accessed directly.

```
........................................................oxtut9e
#include <oxstd.h>

class MySimula
{
    decl m_cT;              // sample size
    decl m_cRep;            // no of replications
    decl m_mCoefVal;        // coeff.values of each replication

    MySimula(const cT, const cM); // constructor
    Simulate();             // do the experiment
    Report();               // print simulation results
};
MySimula::MySimula(const cT, const cM)
{
    m_cRep = cM;
    m_cT = cT;
}
MySimula::Simulate()
{
    decl i;

    for (i = 0; i < m_cRep; ++i)
    {
        // do the replication
    }
    Report();
}
MySimula::Report()
{
    print("Did nothing ", m_cRep, " times\n");
}

main()
{
    decl mysim;

    mysim = new MySimula(50, 1000);

    mysim->Simulate();
    delete mysim;
}
........................................................
```

▶[9.9] Try the modified program. Add a Generate() function to the class; this should be called from within the replication loop, and have two arguments: the replication number, and the sample size.

9.4.3 Inheritance

The base class MySimula is intended to remain unaware of the actual experiment. To simulate the drawings from the normal distribution, create a SimNormal class deriving from MySimula. The one difference from C++ is that the constructor of the base class is *not* automatically called, so we must call it explicitly from the SimNormal constructor. We assume that you did the previous exercise, and created the same Generate() in MySimula as present in SimNormal:

.... *oxtut9f*

```
// ...
// code for MySimula is unchanged
// apart from addition of Generate();

class SimNormal : MySimula
{
    SimNormal(const cT, const cM); // constructor
    Generate(const iRep, const cT);
};
SimNormal::SimNormal(const cT, const cM)
{
    MySimula(cT, cM);      // call base class constructor
}
SimNormal::Generate(const iRep, const cT)
{
}

main()
{
    dccl mysim;

    mysim = new SimNormal(50, 1000);

    mysim->Simulate();
    delete mysim;
}
```
....

▶[9.10] Reduce the number of replications to 2. In MySimula's Generate() add a line printing 'MySimula::Generate()'. In SimNormal's Generate() a line printing 'SimNormal::Generate()'. When you run this, the output will indicate that it is MySimula's version which is called.

9.4.4 Virtual functions

The previous exercise showed that we have not achieved our aim yet: the wrong Generate() is called.

▶[9.11] In the MySimula class declaration replace
```
        Generate(const iRep, const cT);
```

with

```
        virtual Generate(const iRep, const cT);
```

and rerun the program. Did you see the difference?

So, adding the `virtual` keyword to the function declaration in MySimula solved the problem: the generator of the derived class is called. There was no need to do the same for the `Generate()` function in SimNormal (but there is if we wish to derive from SimNormal and replace its `Generate()` yet again).

What if MySimula wishes to call its own `Generate()`? In that case, prefix it with `MySimula::`, so that the loop body reads:

```
        MySimula::Generate(i, m_cT);
```

SimNormal can have access to MySimula's `Generate()` in the same way.

9.4.5 Last step

That really is all we need to know from object-oriented programming to finish this project. It remains to fill in the actual procedures. Of course, the preprogrammed Simulation class is much more advanced, but therefore a bit harder to use.

▶[9.12] Perhaps you should try to complete the program yourself first. If you got stuck along the way, the code up to the previous exercise is provided as *oxtut9y.ox*.

9.5 Conclusion

Ox only implements a subset of the object-oriented facilities in C++. This avoids the complexity of C++, while retaining the most important functionality.

Several useful packages for Ox are downloadable. Often these derive from the Database class, as for example the Arfima (for estimating and forecasting fractionally integrated models) and DPD packages (for estimating dynamic panel data models). You can look at these to learn more about object-oriented programming. In addition, these classes can easily be plugged into a simulation class. So, once the estimation side is done, the Monte Carlo experimentation can be started very rapidly. And, no global variables: you can use several objects at once, without any possibility of unexpected side effects.

The next chapter will apply the object-oriented features to develop a small package for probit estimation.

Chapter 10

Example: probit estimation

10.1 Introduction

In this chapter all the principles of the previous chapters are applied to develop procedures for probit estimation. The theory is briefly reviewed, and then applied to write programs of increasing sophistocation. Four version of the program are developed:

(1) Maximum likelihood estimation, numerical derivatives, using global variables along the lines of §4.9.
(2) Addition of analytical first derivatives, numerical computation of standard errors.
(3) Avoid global variables by using a class.
(4) Create a more sophisticated class.
(5) Use the class in a Monte Carlo experiment.

10.2 The probit model

Several earlier examples involved least squares estimation, where it is assumed that the dependent variable is continuous. A discrete choice model is one where the dependent variable denotes a category, so it is discrete and not continuous. This section briefly reviews the application of maximum likelihood estimation to such models. General references are Cramer (1991), McFadden (1984) and Amemiya (1981) among others.

An example of a categorical dependent variable is:

$$y_i = 0 \quad \text{if household } i \text{ owns no car,}$$
$$y_i = 1 \quad \text{otherwise.}$$

This example is a binary choice problem: there are two categories and the dependent variable is a dummy variable. With a discrete dependent variable, interest lies in modelling the probabilities of observing a certain outcome. Write

$$p_i = \mathsf{P}\left\{y_i = 1\right\}.$$

To test our programs we use the data from Finney (1947), provided in the files `finney.in7` and `finney.bn7` (in the `ox/samples/maximize` folder but also

71

supplied with the tutorial files). This data set holds 39 observations on the occurrence of vaso-constriction (the dummy variable, called 'vaso') in the skin of the fingers after taking a single deep breath. The dose is measured by the volume of air inspired ('volume') and the average rate of inspiration ('rate'). Some graphs of the data are given in Hendry and Doornik (1996, Ch. 9).

Applying OLS to these data has several disadvantages here. First, it doesn't yield proper probabilities, as it is not restricted to lie between 0 and 1 (OLS is called the linear probability model: $p_i = x_i'\beta$). Secondly, the disturbances cannot be normally distributed, as they only take on two values: $\epsilon_i = 1 - p_i$ or $\epsilon_i = 0 - p_i$. Finally, they are also heteroscedastic: $E[\epsilon_i] = (1 - p_i)p_i + (0 - p_i)(1 - p_i) = 0$, $E[\epsilon_i^2] = (1 - p_i)^2 p_i + (0 - p_i)^2(1 - p_i) = (1 - p_i)p_i$.

A simple solution is to introduce an underlying continuous variable y_i^*, which is not observed. Observed is instead:

$$y_i = \begin{cases} 0 & \text{if } y_i^* < 0, \\ 1 & \text{if } y_i^* \geq 0. \end{cases} \tag{10.1}$$

Now we can introduce explanatory variables:

$$y_i^* = x_i'\beta - \epsilon_i.$$

and write

$$p_i = \mathsf{P}\{y_i = 1\} = \mathsf{P}\{x_i'\beta - \epsilon_i \geq 0\} = F_\epsilon(x_i'\beta).$$

Observations with $y_i = 1$ contribute p_i to the likelihood, observations with $y_i = 0$ contribute $1 - p_i$:

$$L(\beta \mid X) = \prod_{\{y_i=0\}} (1 - p_i) \prod_{\{y_i=1\}} p_i, \tag{10.2}$$

and the log-likelihood becomes:

$$\ell(\beta \mid X) = \sum_{i=1}^{N} [(1 - y_i)\log(1 - p_i) + y_i \log p_i] = \sum_{i=1}^{N} \ell_i(\beta). \tag{10.3}$$

The choice of F_ϵ determines the method. Using the logistic distribution leads to *logit* (which is analytically simpler than probit). The standard normal distribution gives *probit*. Writing $\Phi(z)$ for the standard normal probablity at z:

$$p_i = \Phi(x_i'\beta).$$

As explained in §4.7, we choose to maximize ℓ/N, rather than ℓ.

10.3 Step 1: estimation

```
.......................................................... probit1
#include <oxstd.h>
#import <maximize>

decl g_mY;                                      // global data
decl g_mX;                                      // global data

fProbit(const vP, const adFunc, const avScore,
    const amHessian)
{
    decl prob = probn(g_mX * vP);    // vP is column vector

    adFunc[0] = double(
        meanc(g_mY .* log(prob) + (1-g_mY) .* log(1-prob)));

return 1;                               // 1 indicates success
}

main()
{
    decl vp, dfunc, ir;

    print("Probit example 1, run on ", date(), ".\n\n");

    decl mx = loadmat("data/finney.in7");

    g_mY = mx[][0];          // dependent variable: 0,1 dummy
    g_mX = 1 ~ mx[][3:4]; // regressors: 1, Lrate, Lvolume
    delete mx;

    vp = <-0.465; 0.842; 1.439>;          // starting values

    MaxControl(-1, 1);                 // print each iteration
                                               // maximize
    ir = MaxBFGS(fProbit, &vp, &dfunc, 0, TRUE);

    print("\n", MaxConvergenceMsg(ir),
        " using numerical derivatives",
        "\nFunction value = ", dfunc * rows(g_mY),
        "; parameters:", vp);
}
..........................................................
```

We can discuss this program from top to bottom. First, in addition to oxstd.h, we need to include the maximize.h header file, and link in the maximization code (cf. §4.8).

The likelihood function is set up as in §4.7, forcing us to use global variables: the $N \times 1$ matrix Y, containing only zeros and ones, and the $N \times k$ matrix X which holds the regressors.

fProbit() evaluates the log-likelihood $\ell(\beta)$ at the provided parameter values (vP holds β as a column vector). The function value is returned in the dFunc argument (see §2.8.5). The fProbit() function itself returns a 1 when it succeeds, and should return a 0 otherwise.

The probabilities $p_i = \Phi(x_i'\beta)$ are computed in one statement, because all the observations are stacked:

$$P = \begin{pmatrix} p_1 \\ \vdots \\ p_N \end{pmatrix} = \Phi(X\beta).$$

All the likelihoods can also be computed in one step as

$$(1 - Y) \ .^* \ \log(1 - P) + Y \ .^* \ \log(P).$$

The resulting $N \times 1$ vector is summed using sumc(). This returns a 1×1 matrix, which is converted to a double using the double() typecast function.

This takes us to the main() function. Here the first step is to load the data matrix into the variable mx. The first column is the y variable, which is stored in g_mY. The fourth and fifth (remember: indexing starts at zero) are concatenated with a 1 to create a constant term (cf. §2.4), this is stored in g_mX. Now mx is not needed anymore, and delete is used to remove its contents from memory.

Starting values have been chosen on the basis of a prior linear regression, using scaled OLS coefficients: $2.5\beta_{OLS} - 1.25$ for the constant term, and $2.5\beta_{OLS}$ for the remaining coefficients. MaxControl leaves the maximum number of iterations unchanged, but ensures that the results of each iteration is printed out. Initially that is useful, but as the program gets better, we shall want to switch that off again.

We do not meed to specify the initial (inverse) Hessian matrix for MaxBFGS. The argument 0 makes it use the identity matrix, which is the usual starting 'curvature' measure for BFGS. As the maximization process proceeds, that matrix will converge to the true (inverted) Hessian matrix. Also, the matrix on output is not useful for computing standard errors: imagine starting with the identity matrix, from the optimum values. Then the procedure will converge immediately, and the output matrix will still be the identity matrix.

Finally, when MaxBFGS() is finished, it returns the status of the final results as an integer. These are predefined constants, and can be translated to a text message using MaxConvergenceMsg(). Hopefully the return value is MAX_CONV, corresponding to strong convergence.

The maximization converges quickly (the number of iterations depend on convergence criteria and on whether you used ℓ or ℓ/n), with output (the first iterations have been omitted):

```
Probit example 1, run on  1-12-1997.

Position after 13 BFGS iterations
```

```
Status: Strong convergence
parameters
        -1.5039          2.5117          2.8611
gradients
 -3.5936e-005 -1.7996e-005  2.2059e-005
function value =       -0.375475160739

Strong convergence using numerical derivatives
Function value = -14.6435; parameters:
        -1.5039
         2.5117
         2.8611
```

10.4 Step 2: Analytical scores

Computing analytical scores requires differentiating the log-likelihood with respect to β. This can be done inside the summation in (10.3):

$$\frac{\partial \ell_i(\beta)}{\partial \beta_k} = (1 - y_i) \left(\frac{-1}{1 - p_i}\right) \frac{\partial p_i}{\partial \beta_k} + (y_i) \left(\frac{1}{p_i}\right) \frac{\partial p_i}{\partial \beta_k} = \frac{y_i - p_i}{(1 - p_i)p_i} \frac{\partial p_i}{\partial \beta_k}.$$

The derivative of the normal probability is the normal density:

$$\frac{\partial p_i}{\partial \beta_k} = \frac{\partial \Phi(x_i'\beta)}{\partial \beta_k} = \phi(x_i'\beta)x_{ik}.$$

As for the log-likelihood, the full factor multiplying x_{ik} can be computed in one go for all individuals:

$$W = (Y - P) \ .\!^\star \ \phi \ ./\ ((1 - P) \ .\!^\star \ P).$$

W is an $N \times 1$ vector which has to be multiplied by each $x_{.k}$ to obtain the three score values for each individual log-likelihood. Again, one multiplication will do:

$$S = W \ .\!^\star \ X.$$

This uses the 'tabular' form of multiplication (§3.4): all three columns of X are multiplied by the one column in W; the resulting S is an $N \times 3$ matrix. Then summing up each column and dividing by N gives the derivatives of the complete scaled log-likelihood. Because MaxBFGS expects a column vector, this has to be transposed.

....*part of probit2*

```
fProbit(const vP, const adFunc, const avScore,
    const amHessian)
{
    decl prob = probn(g_mX * vP);    // vP is column vector
    decl tail = 1 - prob;
```

```
adFunc[0] = double(
    meanc(g_mY .* log(prob) + (1-g_mY) .* log(tail)));

if (avScore)                        // if !0: compute score
{
    decl weight = (g_mY - prob) .* densn(g_mX * vP)
        ./ (prob .* tail);
    avScore[0] = meanc(weight .* g_mX)';// need column
}

return 1;                           // 1 indicates success
}
```

The analytical derivatives are more accurate than the numerical ones. A small difference may just be noted when comparing the final gradients of the two programs.

The final program also computes estimated standard errors of the coefficients using numerical second derivatives of the log-likelihood at the converged parameter values:

....*part of probit2*
```
                // if converged: compute standard errors
if (ir == MAX_CONV || ir == MAX_WEAK_CONV)
{
    if (Num2Derivative(fProbit, vp, &mhess))
    {
        decl mcovar = -invert(mhess) / cn;
        print("standard errors:", sqrt(diagonal(mcovar)'));
    }
}
```

These are only computed when there is convergence. The complete estimated variance-covariance matrix is minus the inverse of the second derivatives:

$$\widehat{V_1[\hat{\beta}]} = -Q(\hat{\beta})^{-1}, \quad \text{where } Q = \frac{\partial^2 \ell}{\partial \beta \partial \beta'}.$$

The standard errors are the square root of the diagonal of that matrix. Another way of computing the variance can be obtained from the outer product of the gradients (OPG):

$$\widehat{V_2[\hat{\beta}]} = (S'S)^{-1}.$$

▶[10.1] Adjust fProbit in such a way that it returns $S'S$ in the amHessian argument. Use this to compare the two variance estimates. The result should be approximately:

```
standard errors:        0.63740      0.93635      0.90793
OPG standard errors:    0.59988      1.1910       1.0142
```

10.5 Step 3: removing global variables

Step 3 uses the object-oriented techniques of Chapter 9 to remove the global variables. The Database class is used to derive from in order to facilitate data loading. The code listed illustrates by omitting that part of the program which is nearly identical to the previous program (apart from the switch from g_mY, g_mX to m_mY, m_mX):

```
.............................................. outline of probit3
#include <oxstd.h>
#import <database>
#import <maximize>

class Probit : Database
{
    decl m_mY;                 /* dependent variable [cT][1] */
    decl m_mX;         /* regressor data vector [cT][m_cX] */

    Probit();                               /* constructor */
    Estimate();                       /* does the estimation */
    fProbit(const vP, const adFunc, const avScore,
        const amHessian);           /* log-likelihood */
};

Probit::Probit()
{
    this.Database();              // intialize base class
    print("Probit class example 3, object created on ",
        date(), ".\n\n");
}
Probit::fProbit(const vP, const adFunc, const avScore,
    const amHessian)
{
//...... as before, using m_mY, m_mX instead of g_mY, g_mX
}
Probit::Estimate()
{
//as main() before, using m_mY, m_mX instead of g_mY, g_mX
}

main()
{
    decl probitobj;
                    // create an object of class Probit
    probitobj = new Probit();
                    // load the data, estimate the model
    probitobj.Estimate();

    delete probitobj;                  // done with object
}
..............................................................
```

The Probit class derived from the Database class. It adds two data members for Y and X, and three functions:

(1) The constructor to call the base class constructor and print a message.
(2) The loglikelihood function.
(3) The Estimate() function contains the code which was previously in main():
loading the data, estimating and then printing the results.

The new main() creates the object, calls Estimate(), and deletes the object.

10.6 Step 4: using names of variables

The version of Step 3 has a serious defect: for each new model formulation the Estimate() function must be modified. Ideally, the code of the class works for any binary probit model, and not just for this one. Modifications to achieve this take us close to the approach taken in packages such as Arfima and DPD.

First, the old Probit::Estimate() is split in three parts: InitData(), Estimate() and Output. The Database class has the facility to store a model formulation, which is used in this step.

The resulting program is used in a similar way to the PcFiml example in §9.2. The full listing is in probit4.ox. Here is the main() function:

```
................................................part of probit4
main()
{
    decl probitobj;

    probitobj = new Probit();

                             // load data file into object
    probitobj.LoadIn7("data/finney.in7");
    probitobj.Info();               // print database summary
    probitobj.Deterministic(FALSE);     // create constant

                             // Formulate the model
    probitobj.Select(Y_VAR, { "vaso",0,0 } );
    probitobj.Select(X_VAR, { "Constant",0,0,
        "Lrate",0,0, "Lvolume",0,0 } );
    probitobj.SetSelSample(-1, 1, -1, 1);   // full sample

    MaxControl(-1, 1);               // print each iteration
    probitobj.Estimate(<-0.465; 0.842; 1.439>);// maximize

    delete probitobj;
}
................................................
```

10.7 A Monte Carlo experiment

One of the claims we made was that, once wrapped up in a class, it is easier to reuse the code. To make our case, we round off with a Monte Carlo experiment of Probit estimation. Once again several steps are involved.

All files in this section are bprobit.* and bpro*.*, where the b stands for binomial.

10.7.1 Split source code

The probit4.ox file contains class header, class content and main() all in one file. To make it generally useful, this has to be split in three files:

- bprobit.h – class header file,
- bprobit.ox – class implementation file,
- bprotest.ox – main (left overs from probit4.ox).

The header file has one interesting feature:

....*part of bprobit.h*
```
#ifndef BPROTEST_INCLUDED
#define BPROTEST_INCLUDED

// class definition

#endif // BPROTEST_INCLUDED
```
....

This prevents the header file from being included more than once in a source code file (necessary because a class can de defined only once). So if you now write in your code file:
```
#include "bprobit.h"
#include "bprobit.h"
```
Then the first time BPROTEST_INCLUDED is not defined, and the full file is included. The second time BPROTEST_INCLUDED is defined, and the part between #ifndef and #endif is skipped.

The bprobit.h file already imports database and maximize, which then is not needed in the main code anymore as long as bprobit.h is included. The top of bprotest.ox includes bprobit.h, but also the Ox file directly (as this file is still under development at this stage, it is inconvenient to create a precompiled (.oxo) file, but at a later stage that might be a good idea):

....*part of bprotest.ox*
```
#include <oxstd.h>
#include "bprobit.h"
#include "bprobit.ox"
```
....

10.7.2 Extending the class

A few extensions are required to make the class more useful. When working from someone elses class, this is best done by deriving our custom version from it through inheritance. Here we have control over the class (which is still quite basic), and add the functions directly:

- `SetPrint(const fPrint)` – to switch automatic printing on/off,
- `IsConverged()` – to check for convergence after estimation,
- `GetParameters()` – returns estimated parameters,
- `GetStandardErrors()` – returns estimated standard errors of parameters.

In addition, `GetStandardErrors()` and `IsConverged()` are now used in `Output()`, and `Estimate()` returns the `MaxBFGS()` code.

10.7.3 One replication

Continuing with the step-wise refinement of the program, we start with a one-replication experiment. Instead of loading a datafile, and formulating a model specific to that data, we need to create artificial data ourselves:

```
............................................................. bprosim1.ox
#include <oxstd.h>
#include "bprobit.h"
#include "bprobit.ox"

main()
{
    decl probitobj, ct = 100, x, y;

    probitobj = new Probit();                   // create object

    probitobj.Create(1, 1, 1, ct, 1);   // create database
    probitobj.Deterministic(FALSE);     // create constant

    x = ranu(ct, 1);                            // artificial x
    y = 1 + x + rann(ct, 1);                    // artificial y
    y = y .< 1 .? 0 .: 1;       // translate into 0,1 variable
    probitobj.Append(x ~ y, {"x", "y"});// extend database
    probitobj.Info();              // print database summary

                            // formulate the model: y on 1,x
    probitobj.Select(Y_VAR, { "y",0,0 } );
    probitobj.Select(X_VAR, { "Constant",0,0, "x",0,0 } );
    probitobj.SetSelSample(-1, 1, -1, 1);    // full sample

    probitobj.Estimate(<0; 0>);                 // maximize

    delete probitobj;
}
.....................................................................
```

▶[10.2] Run this program for various sample sizes. An experiment like this can be useful to check your coding if you use a large sample size (assuming that the estimator is consistent): the obtained parameters should be reasonably close to the input values. For $N = 100\,000$ we found:

```
parameters      standard errors
-0.0010194          0.0080956
  1.0087            0.014805
```

Can you explain why the constant term is insignificant?

10.7.4 Many replications

Most of the work is done now. What remains is to create a replication loop, and accumulate the results.

- Parameter estimates and their standard errors are stored by appending the results to `params` and `parses` respectively. This starts from an empty matrix (starting from 0 adds a column of zeros and affects the outcomes).
- The x variable is kept fixed, but the y is recreated at every experiment. It is stored in the database of the probit object, from where the estimation function will retrieve it.
- The results are only stored when the estimation was successful. Especially when numerical optimization is used, is it important to take into account that estimation can fail. Here we reject the experiment, and try again, until `crep` experiments have succeeded (if they all fail, the program would go in an infinite loop).
- At the end, a report is printed out.

```
. . . . . . . . . . . . . . . . . . . . . . . . . . . . . . . . . . . . . . . . . . . . . . . . . . . . . . . . . . . . bprosim2.ox
#include <oxstd.h>
#include "bprobit.h"

#include "bprobit.ox"

main()
{
    decl probitobj, ct = 100, x, y, crep = 100, irep,
        ires, cfailed, params, parses;

    probitobj = new Probit();
    probitobj.Create(1, 1, 1, ct, 1);      // create database
    probitobj.Deterministic(FALSE);        // create constant

    x = ranu(ct, 1);                  // fixed during experiment
    y = zeros(ct, 1); // 0 as yet, created in replications
    probitobj.Append(x ~ y, {"x", "y"});

    probitobj.Select(Y_VAR, { "y",0,0 } );    // formulate
    probitobj.Select(X_VAR, { "Constant",0,0, "x",0,0 } );
    probitobj.SetSelSample(-1, 1, -1, 1);    // full sample
```

```
probitobj.SetPrint(FALSE);     // no intermediate output

params = parses = <>;
for (irep = cfailed = 0; irep < crep; )
{
    y = 1 + x + rann(ct, 1);   // create new y variable
    y = y .< 1 .? 0 .: 1;              // make into 0,1
    probitobj.Renew(y, {"y"});  // replace in database

    ires = probitobj.Estimate(<0; 0>);

    if (!probitobj.IsConverged())
    {
        ++cfailed;                 // count no of failures
        continue;         // failed: reject and try again
    }
    params ~= probitobj.GetParameters();        // store
    parses ~= probitobj.GetStandardErrors();
    ++irep;                           // next replication
}

println("No of successful replications: ",
    crep, " (", cfailed, " failed)");
println("Sample size: ", ct);
println("estimated parameters",
    "%c", {"mean-par", "sd-par", "mean-se", "sd-se"},
    meanr(params) ~ sqrt(varr(params)) ~
    meanr(parses) ~ sqrt(varr(parses)));

delete probitobj;
}
```
....

▶[10.3] For $M = 100, N = 100$ we obtained:
```
No of successful replications: 100 (0 failed)
Sample size: 100
estimated parameters
          mean-par        sd-par       mean-se          sd-se
         -0.013406       0.25857       0.24224      0.0039480
           1.0671        0.46142       0.46980       0.021313
```
Interpret these results.

▶[10.4] Implement a procedure which automatically generates starting values.

▶[10.5] Derive and implement analytical second derivatives.

▶[10.6] Modify the program to use the simulation class for the Monte Carlo experimentation.

▶[10.7] In (10.2) the 0–1 variable y_i is used as a selection variable, whereas in (10.3)
this selection is implemented through multiplication by 0 or 1. Can you find the

(extreme) situations in which this is not the same (hint: compute the value of $0 \times \inf$)?

▶[10.8] Extend the program to print the time it took to complete the Monte Carlo experiment.

10.8 Conclusion

If you made it this far you have certainly become an *oxpert* (to quote from van der Sluis, 1997). From now on we hope that you can spend less time on learning the computing language, and more on the econometric or statistical content of the problems you intend to solve. We wish you productive use of the Ox programming language.

Appendix A1

Installation Issues

A1.1 Updating the environment

Skip this section if you managed to run the Ox programs in this booklet. Otherwise, you probably still have to update the PATH and OXPATH environment variable.

The executable (ox1.exe etc.) is in the ox\bin folder, for example by default it is in:

```
C:\Program files\Ox\bin
```

So, update your PATH variable if necessary. Also, the oxpath environment variable must be set to the ox\include; ox folders, for example:[1]

```
set OXPATH=C:\Program files\Ox\include;C:\Program files\Ox
```

Without these, you can still run myfirst.ox, but a lot of typing is needed:

```
"C:\Program files\Ox\bin\oxl"
        "-iC:\Program files\Ox\include" myfirst.ox
```

The double quotes are required because of the space in the file name (under Windows 3.1, Program files would be ProgramF).

A1.2 Using the OxEdit editor

OxEdit is a powerful text editor, and a very useful program in its own right. OxEdit has some features which are especially useful when writing Ox programs:

- Syntax colouring
  Three colours are used to distinguish keywords, constants and comment. This makes the code more readable, and mistakes easier to spot.
- Facility to easily comment in or comment out blocks of text
- Run Ox programs from inside OxEdit

---

[1]In Windows 3.1 and 95 the PATH and OXPATH variables are set by editing the autoexec.bat file. In Windows NT, you can do it using the Control panel, System: use the environment page in the system properties.

The screen capture shows OxEdit with `myfirst.ox` after running it from the Modules menu.

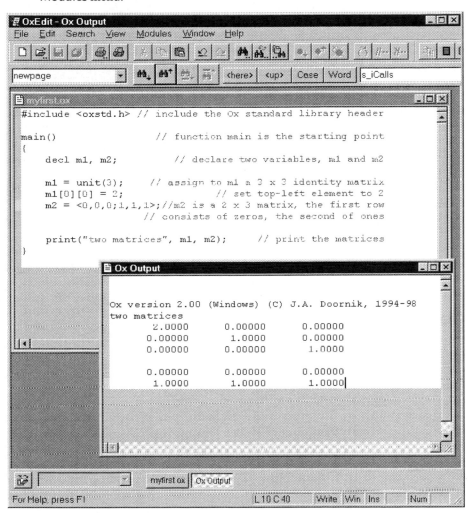

The first time you use OxEdit, execute the Add Ox modules command on the Modules menu. From then on you can run your Ox programs without leaving OxEdit:

- Ox - runs the currently active document window using `ox1.exe`. The output will appear in the window called Ox Output.
- OxRun - runs the currently active document window using *OxRun*. The output will appear in `GiveWin`.
- Ox - interactive - starts an interactive session. The input/output window is called Session.ox.

– Ox - d̲ebug - starts a debug session for the currently active document window. The input/output window is called Debug.ox.

You can even add a button representing Ox on the toolbar: right click on the toolbar (in the area next to a button), and add the relevant tool to the toolbar. You might need a few separators at the end to avoid a partial button.

References

Amemiya, T. (1981). Qualitative response models: A survey, *Journal of Economic Literature*, **19**, 1483–1536.

Cramer, J. S. (1986). *Econometric Applications of Maximum Likelihood Methods*. Cambridge: Cambridge University Press.

Cramer, J. S. (1991). *The LOGIT Model: An Introduction for Economists*. London: Edward Arnold.

Davidson, R. and MacKinnon, J. G. (1993). *Estimation and Inference in Econometrics*. New York: Oxford University Press.

Doornik, J. A. (1998). *Object-Oriented Matrix Programming using Ox*. London: Timberlake Consultants.

Finney, D. J. (1947). The estimation from individual records of the relationship between dose and quantal response, *Biometrika*, **34**, 320–334.

Fletcher, R. (1987). *Practical Methods of Optimization* 2nd edition. New York: John Wiley & Sons.

Gill, P. E., Murray, W. and Wright, M. H. (1981). *Practical Optimization*. New York: Academic Press.

Hendry, D. F. (1995). *Dynamic Econometrics*. Oxford: Oxford University Press.

Hendry, D. F. and Doornik, J. A. (1996). *Empirical Econometric Modelling using PcGive 9 for Windows*. London: International Thomson Business Press.

Judge, G. G., Hill, R. C., Griffiths, W. E., Lütkepohl, H. and Lee, T.-C. (1988). *Introduction to the Theory and Practice of Econometrics* 2nd edition. New York: John Wiley.

McFadden, D. L. (1984). Econometric analysis of qualitative response models, In Griliches, Z. and Intriligator, M. D. (eds.), *Handbook of Econometrics*, Vol. 2–3, Ch. 24. Amsterdam: North-Holland.

Press, W. H., Flannery, B. P., Teukolsky, S. A. and Vetterling, W. T. (1988). *Numerical Recipes in C*. New York: Cambridge University Press.

Ripley, B. D. (1987). *Stochastic Simulation*. New York: John Wiley & Sons.

Thisted, R. A. (1988). *Elements of Statistical Computing. Numerical Computation*. New York: Chapman and Hall.

van der Sluis, P. J. (1997). EmmPack 1.0: C/C++ code for use with Ox for estimation of univariate stochastic volatility models with the efficient method of moments, Tinbergen institute discussion paper TI97-?/4, University of Amsterdam.

Subject Index